The Ethics of Civilization

The Ethics of Civilization

Arnold H. Kamiat

Author of "The Critique of Poor Reason"
and "Social Forces in Personality Stunting"

Public Affairs Press
WASHINGTON, D. C.

This is a book about the "civilizers"—and a plea for more of them. As the author writes: "Their ranks are open to everyone"; and blessed be those who enter the ranks. The health of our human society depends upon these few, for they create and sustain the great values of life.

We, in all the ranks of life, need to learn what a "civilizer" looks like—how he thinks and acts; how he refuses to think and act; how, in short, he goes at the whole baffling business of living. Learning the way of the civilized mind, we may act in like manner and thus keep from slipping into the ranks of the barbarians.

This is the upshot of this wise and revealing book. It is written for those who prefer not to slip.

HARRY A. OVERSTREET

INTRODUCTION

There exists a minority group which is perhaps the most important of all minorities. It is the minority made up of the men and women who create or sustain ethical, aesthetic, intellectual or religious values, and who actively pursue these values before all else. These people are deviants. They deviate from the norm—i.e., the statistical norm— but this does not worry them. What they are most anxious about is the task of living up to civilized norms: the norms of ethics, art, intellect and religion. These are the norms from which they do not deviate.

Every civilized society has had its minority of civilizers. It is they who create civilizations; they who, more than anyone else, sustain them. They have been doing this for thousands of years. They have done this in peace and in war, in prosperity and in depression, during revolution and counter-revolution, and in the face of opposition and persecution. And yet the civilizers have been constantly and contemptuously scorned as impractical and unrealistic. Today it is the fashion to dub them escapists, people who are fleeing from life. But this is fallacy. Those who pursue, create, appreciate, and sustain life's highest values cannot be charged with running away from life.

Today the position of the civilizers is a precarious one in a great many parts of the globe. After millennia of civilization, the world still does not know who its real builders and sustainers are. It still scorns the civilizers as impractical and unrealistic deviants. It does not understand them. Not understanding them, it fears them. In every age and in every nation, they have been accused of heresy because they are always coming forward with questions and inquiries and criticisms and new ideas. They are always upsetting the status quo and everybody's comfort and peace of mind.

The civilizers are particularly obnoxious to autocrats, tyrants, dictators, totalitarians and oligarchs of all kinds and hues. It is simply impossible to keep a party line straight with the civilizers around. And so today in many parts of the world the civilizers have become objects of persecution. Today in many places their lot is that of the refugee, the exile, the martyr.

The crisis that civilization faces today is one that the civilizers must help solve. Deeply cherished values are in jeopardy, and it is the

v

civilizers who are called upon to rescue them, for it is they who have created them and who, more than any one else, have in the past sustained them. It is they who must create the ideas and bring into being the social institutions and systems that will make it possible for men and women to grow up and lead full and happy lives. It is they who must furnish the outlines for the kind of society and way of life that will breed more civilizers. The two criteria by means of which the worth and greatness of a society are to be judged are the degree of psychological maturity exhibited by its constituent individuals and the number of civilizers to be found among them and their contributions to the store of civilized values. A society ranking high according to the first standard would rank high according to the second.

This book is therefore a call to civilizers. There are things for them to do, things that they should and must do.

To many the things that this book says about the civilizers will have an undemocratic sound. In actual fact the position taken is democratic. The civilizers constitute a democratic aristocracy. Their ranks are open to everyone. Any man and any woman, of whatever nation or ethnic group or class or church, can make the ascent to the level of civilizer. No formalities are involved. All that is necessary is that one shall pursue, actively and primarily, the values called ethical, aesthetic, intellectual or religious.

*   *   *   *

I take this occasion to thank the editors of *The Humanist* and of *Problems* for permission to include herein several articles that have appeared in their journals. Chapter 2, 4 and 9 are based upon articles in *Problems*; Chapter 6 is a revision of an article in *The Humanist*.

ARNOLD H. KAMIAT

CONTENTS

THE COSMIC TREND

Being seems to subsist on eight levels: inanimate matter, viruses, one-celled organisms, cell colonies, plants, conscious animals, human beings, and civilized human beings.

Roughly, this is equivalent to the course of evolution. Inanimate matter appears to be the first stage. Whether viruses or one-celled organisms constitute the next stage is a question. But then it is a question whether life evolves out of matter. It may be that matter and life are coeval, with life emerging into empirically apprehensible forms when conditions are favorable. Materialists to the contrary notwithstanding, there appears to be a wide gap between life and matter. Evolution, if it does take place here, makes a jump—although the virus may constitute an intermediate stage. Some viruses, however, seem to be parasitic and make their home in cellular tissue. These may or may not constitute a stage coeval with or later than the cell.

From one-celled organisms to cell colonies is a small step. The step from cell colony to plant is also comparatively small. But when the first conscious animal appears, evolution takes a tremendous jump. The gap between the non-conscious cell colony and plant, on the one hand, and the conscious animal on the other, is great indeed. Moreover, it is perhaps wrong to speak of consciousness evolving from the non-conscious. It may well be that consciousness is coeval with life, or with matter and life, and that it manifests itself on the animal level when conditions are favorable.

Evolution seems to take another jump when humanity appears. There is nothing in animals other than human that suggests the capacity to form, entertain, and communicate concepts. Like the living cell and the conscious animal, the concept-forming human appears to be an emergent novelty. Is it proper to speak of life, consciousness and concept-formation as emergents? Whether they emerge from antecedent states or are newly created it is difficult to say. But there they are and they are real.

The human race does not, however, represent the latest stage of the evolutionary process. The latest is that represented by that minority of humans who can be called the makers and sustainers of civilization because they are the men and women who create or sustain four classes of value: ethical, intellectual, aesthetic, religious. In this group one finds prophets, ethical and social reformers, artists, philosophers and scientists, as well as those who deeply and persistently appreciate the values these create. Not all reformers, artists, philosophers and scientists are to be included here. Excluded are the artists, philosophers and scientists who deliberately peddle falsehoods, prostitute their talents, flatter their readers or hearers, and all for the sake of money or power or to give expression to some neurotic or psychotic impulse. Excluded also are the revolutionists and counter-revolutionists who, for exactly similar reasons, destroy the greatest values there are. Also excluded are many members of the priesthood of all the world's churches. They have in all times and places sacrificed religious values, subordinating them to ritual, myth and the need for perpetuating vested interests, ecclesiastical and otherwise.

To put it clearly and briefly, what is thus far on this earth the highest stage of evolution is constituted by a small minority composed of those who actively and persistently pursue ethical, aesthetic, intellectual and/or religious values in preference to material, political or biological ones. They do not necessarily neglect these secondary values, but they do not make them the goals of living.

This minority can be said to constitute a spiritual aristocracy, the only kind of aristocracy worth while.

                              *   *   *   *

These, then, appear to be the stages of evolution. This may, however, be only an appearance. It may or may not be a case of each stage growing or emerging out of an antecedent one. As has been suggested, matter and life, or matter, life and consciousness may be coeval, with life and consciousness emerging when conditions are favorable.

Whether all this is the expression of some sort of cosmic urge, a nisus toward civilization, it is not possible to say. Nor is it possible to determine whether each stage comes into being in order that subsequent stages might be. But some sort of evolution or development has taken place, and the direction it has taken is unmistakeable. Intended or unintended, the stage of civilized values has on this earth and for some people been attained. Then perhaps this earth is not so insignificant a planet after all. And the people in question—the civilizers—are not insignificant either. They constitute the one group that can boast that it occupies the highest level of being, and without inviting the charge of collective egotism. They do appear to be in a sense a chosen people.

The civilizers have never had an easy time. Struggle has been their lot. They have always been in the minority. They have seldom been understood by the majority. Whenever and wherever they have come forward with new ideas, they have been the objects of scorn, contempt, fear, hate and persecution. They have had to wage a persistent struggle against the majority. This struggle is perhaps the most basic of all class wars.

A BASIC CLASS STRUGGLE

It has become the custom to think of the modern world as peculiarly unspiritual. Other periods, one is assured, were different. Athens, Rome, ancient Israel, ancient India and China, the middle ages, the time of the Reformation, and other epochs, were characterized by a greater emphasis on, and wider participation in the things of the spirit. The modern period is supposed to have abandoned spirit for materialism, mechanism, industrialism, statism and hedonism.

The frequency with which one comes across this alleged distinction between yesterday and today is appalling. It constitutes a sad commentary, not on the modern world, but on the thought-habits of those philosophers, historians, social scientists, religious leaders and others who accept the distinction as real. One has to deal here with an uncritically accepted stereotype. On the psychological side there appears to be a tendency to disparage one's own generation and to assume the existence in the past of something approaching the golden age of the spirit. This fictive idealization of the past may be a way of castigating one's own age.

The modern world is unspiritual enough, to be sure. But there is no warrant for the assertion that other times were radically different. The fact is that the line is being drawn in the wrong place. The difference is not between periods of time, but between kinds of people. Always there have been those to whom the things of the spirit mattered most; always there have been those to whom these things mattered not so much, or a little, or not at all. The first kind, the civilizers, whom Ignazio Silone calls the seed beneath the snow, has always constituted a sadly small minority; the other kind has made up the rest of humanity. The two groups have waged a persistent struggle, and one that will perhaps continue as long as human society lasts. This class struggle is the one significant conflict; all other struggles are insignificant in comparison. Those between nations, empires, classes, parties and so on, possess no fundamental significance, except to the extent that they affect the life of the spirit. Otherwise, no deep significance attaches to the question of who shall have power, or wealth, or prestige, or territory. These are things prized by children; and all men and women who do not attain to the life of the spirit are indeed children.

Historians reflect a false scale of values. Their histories still give first place to political, economic and military events. But these possess only a secondary importance. Of first and greatest importance is the history of spirit. The latter finds expression in the quest of values of the highest order: religious, ethical, aesthetic and intellectual. Historiography ought therefore to concern itself first of all with accounts of ethical striving, religion, art, science and philosophy. These constitute the empire of the spirit. These are its realm. Of this realm, prophets, saints, martyrs, ethical and social reformers, artists, scientists and philosophers have been the rulers—kings and queens by a more truly divine right. These have been the truly great, great in a big sense. Kings, emperors, politicians, administrators, industrialists, financiers, and military leaders, if they can be considered great at all, have been great in a small sense. Their realms subsist on a level considerably below the spiritual. Leadership on their level is much easier to attain. Persecution is easier than the endurance of martyrdom; the propaganda of falsehood than the pursuit of truth; the perpetuation of squalor than the quest for beauty; inert conservatism than ethical progress; violence than love and good will. One should, for instance, never speak of Alexander the Great, but of Alexander the Little. Nor should one speak of Jesus and Julius Caesar as if they subsisted on the same level. The distance between the two is vast. Jesus is a mountain, Caesar a molehill—greater than most molehills, but still a molehill. Yet historians give first place to kings, emperors, politicians and generals, as if human destiny becomes fulfilled in ruling and being ruled, in sending and being sent into battle.

Yes, there is and always has been a spiritual class struggle. It is a struggle between the vast majority and a pitifully small minority. This is the minority of men and women to whom the things of the spirit are the things that matter. To it, love, good will, magnanimity, kindness, sympathy, justice, truth, reason, art and beauty are the supreme realities. These constitute life for it; these are things to be lived, and lived here and now, not in some far-off Utopia. The things of the spirit may be ultimate, but they are to be lived in the immediate here and the immediate now.

The vast majority of men and women, however, is not greatly interested in ultimates, certainly not in spiritual ultimates. Its interest is rather in things that are immediate in a biological or economic or social sense. True enough, it does not neglect the spiritual entirely.

It is responsive to it in a greater or lesser degree. But its emphasis is on other things. Thus the minority and the majority face each other and carry on a perpetual conflict.

The spiritual minority has long constituted a perplexing problem. In dealing with it, significant alliances have been formed. Radical and conservative, revolutionist and reactionary, exploiter and exploited, master and slave, ruler and subject, priest and atheist, all have stood shoulder to shoulder against prophet and saint, against the seeker after truth. All see in even the lowliest and loneliest of men and women of the spirit a menace to the established order of values. Rightly do they perceive in the spirit a revolutionary force, a truly revolutionary force, far more revolutionary than the superficial thing that wraps itself in the red flag. Its cry, "Woe unto them that are ease in Zion!" always rings in their ears.

The struggle between the civilizers and the unspiritual majority constitutes the most significant, the most fundamental of all conflicts. It is a class struggle that is more far-reaching in its effects than the one that socialists and communists dote upon. The socialist class struggle is a superficial conflict. It is not a war between a higher and a lower set of values; both the contestants share the same values: both aim at power and rule, dominance and wealth. Both appear only too willing to sacrifice the human spirit itself for the sake of victory. The experience of Communist Russia, Nazi Germany, Fascist Italy and Falange Spain shows that the victory of either side represents a defeat for the spirit.

Socialists and communists show little insight when they describe their class struggle as fundamental. Aristotle exhibits profound insight when he speaks of the struggle between good men and those who oppose the good. This struggle is basic. A conflict between contestants who subsist on an unspiritual level cannot be considered fundamental. No matter which side wins, the unspiritual will still be dominant. Hence the socialist class struggle, in spite of all the noise and clamor that surround it, is not as meaningful as those who are engaged in it esteem it to be.

Socialists and communists will, of course, oppose this view. They are certain that they represent a scale of values higher than that of their opponents. They will protest that they fight for humanity, for freedom, for justice, for democracy, and so on. And many of them will maintain this view with all sincerity. They delude themselves. In every struggle, the contestants announce themselves the champions of humanity and the things of the spirit. All parties, all religions, all nations, all classes profess their love for spiritual values. How is it then that the world has always been spiritually such a shambles?

Part of the answer is this: too many people, when they do pursue civilized ends, strive to gain them through the use of *uncivilized means*. They thus betray their spiritual emptiness.

It is a sign of spiritual illiteracy and spiritual immaturity persistently to employ uncivilized means in the pursuit of civilized goals. The spiritually immature make the great and terrible mistake of supposing that the uncivilized can be fought only by a descent to its level. How often has this error led to the most unfortunate consequences!

The spiritually illiterate do not know that civilized ideals must be lived to be realized. Civilized values are generated only by being lived. If there is to be love, one must love. If there is to be sympathy, one must sympathize. When people act justly, there is justice. One cannot depend on liars—or propagandists—to perpetuate truth. There must be artists if there is to be art. Spiritual values do not lie at the end of a long road, to be traversed by unspiritual means. Spirit is not a garment to be put on when the season is ripe for its wearing. It is not something that will come to people sometime in the future when they will in some mysterious way become ready for it. Civilization is a way of life, and therefore must be lived, lived here and lived now, if it is to be real. Spirit is end and spirit is also means—its own means.

* * * *

In its conflict with the unspiritual majority, the spiritual minority relies in the main on spiritual weapons. The persistent reliance on the weapons of the spirit is already a victory for the spirit. Through its employment of such weapons, the spiritual minority is, however, "doomed" to remain a minority. To the majority this proves the minority to be "unrealistic" and "impractical." There are no words in the vocabulary more unintelligently used than the words *realistic* and *practical*. Everyone is always dismissing ideals and proposals on the ground of their alleged unreality and impracticality. Too often the rejection of an idea as unrealistic involves a begging of the question: when the truth of an idea is in question, the nature and characteristics of some slice of reality are still to be determined. Until the determination has been effected, it is sheer presumptuousness to dismiss the idea in question as unrealistic.

Practicality is relative. An action is practical or impractical with reference to the end to which it is related as means. It is impossible to judge of the practicality of an action unless the goal at which it aims is known. The charge of impracticality is often hurled at men and women of the spirit by people who have not taken the trouble

to ascertain the ends the allegedly impractical actions are designed
to subserve.

                    *   *   *   *

Today, as always, the civilized minority is actively applying itself
to the task of generating and preserving life's most precious values.
No contribution that can be made to the resolution of the grave crisis
that confronts modern civilization can possibly be as great, as important, as theirs.   But the crisis that confronts us calls forth from
them efforts of a special kind.   What is required of them is effort in
the direction of revolution—spiritual revolution.   Nothing less than
that can solve the problems which face us today.   The alterations
required are genuinely radical in character.   But the civilized minority
is composed of radicals in the deepest and best sense of the word;
they are also conservatives in the deepest and best sense of that word,
too.   They it is who go to the root of all problems; they it is who
nurture and conserve that which is most worthy of nurture and
conservation.

3

MUST CIVILIZATIONS DIE?

There has been a good deal of discussion among students of civilization concerning what is sometimes referred to as the "law of cycles." According to this "law," civilizations inevitably go through the stages of birth, growth, decline and death. But those who talk of such cycles cling to an outmoded, fatalistic conception of natural law: the notion that natural law decrees what must be. Science knows of no such laws. Science knows only of descriptive, not prescriptive laws. A law simply states that given such and such an antecedent, it is reasonable to expect such and such a consequent. The antecedent itself is not necessarily inevitable. And so, given a society most of the physically adult members of which are in the main ethically, intellectually and aesthetically immature and remain so for decades, generations, centuries, its eventual decline may reasonably be expected. It is, however, not at all essential to a society that any part of its adult population be in any way immature. A society, the physical adults of which are sufficiently mature ethically, intellectually and aesthetically, might conceivably prolong its civilized existence indefinitely. Such a society might be unfortunate enough to be overwhelmed by a barbarian horde, but such a phenomenon requires no law of cycles for its explanation. At any rate, it is time to outgrow the mystagogic conception of natural law as some kind of a cosmic force that decrees and makes this or that event inevitable. Law describes what happens and what may under given circumstances be expected to happen. A law is a description, not a force, except in so far as a description may act as a force. The statement of a law may exert an influence and thus help determine human behavior.

The same considerations apply to another supposed law: the law of catastrophic change. This law "decrees" that social institutions shall become inflexible and rigid, and that when they therefore fail to change in response to new conditions, they shall collapse. The attendant disorder shall be marked by a descent to barbarism, expressed in war, revolution, counter-revolution, dictatorship and social degeneration in all its manifestations. Again, given a society the members of which are sociologically too immature to realize the importance of institutional flexibility and responsiveness to change, given a society most of the members of which subsist on a barbarian level, violent crises accompanied by an intensification of barbarism may reasonably be expected to occur from time to time. But it is no essential part of a society that its members be sociologically immature, or that they subsist on a barbarian level, or that its institutions be inflexible. Conceivably a society of sociologically mature persons would possess institutions responsive to change. Such a society would be in a position to effect even radical changes without any display of barbarism.

It is important to scotch once and for all the antiquated, unscientific, mystagogic conception of natural law as prescriptive and determinative. The laws of nature determine nothing. They only describe. It is things and persons that by their structures and functions determine what the natural laws describing their behavior shall be.

The importance of all this lies in the fact that the espousal of the so-called law of cycles and the so-called law of catastrophic change has dealt the human spirit a blow. It is in part responsible for the fatalism and demoralization of modern times. There are people who pride themselves on their freedom from superstition, people who dismiss the supernatural and who laugh at astrology, and who nonetheless accept the mystagogic notion of a cosmic law or force that has decreed the decline of modern civilization and the rise in the amount of barbarism that is so manifest in the world today. These people do not seem to be in the least aware of their inconsistency. They do not seem to know that they are the victims of superstition and pseudoscience. They have allowed themselves to be spellbound by mystagogues.

Part of the responsibility for this unfortunate situation is to be laid at the door of the scientists themselves. They have not made too much of an effort to educate the lay public in the real meaning of the phrase, *natural law*. In speaking of the latter, they have employed language that, though figurative, is misleading and confusing. They have referred to the laws of nature as "governing." They have described this or that event as occurring in "accordance" with this or that law. They have talked as if they meant to convey the impression that the laws of nature possess causal efficacy. Small wonder that the misconception of natural law as a force, a determiner of events, is so widespread. And if one is tempted to condemn the lay public for its ignorance, one should bear in mind that in this instance it often follows the lead of the scientists and of some philosophers and pseudo-philosophers.

Among the advocates of the "law" of cycles and the "law" of catastrophic change there may be some who will insist that they are anything but mystagogues. Instead, they will claim, they are determinists. Their "law," they will say, is not a force; it is not prescriptive, it is descriptive. What it describes is a cause and effect relationship. There are natural factors that operate to bring civilizations into being, to cause them to grow, and to bring about their decline and extinction. There is, they will say, no mystagogy, no supernaturalism here: only the operation of natural, causal factors.

In reply to them it is but necessary to say that if there are natural factors that make for the birth, growth, decline and death of civilizations, as of course there must be, then every effort must be made to uncover these factors and, if it is at all possible, to manipulate and control them. If such a control is attainable, then the decline and death of civilizations may be taken out of the category of the inevitable.

4

TOWARD ETHICAL TRANSCENDENTALISM

An ethically mature person is one who is able to give and receive love and to enter into democratic and cooperative relations with any other member of the human race, excepting those who are for pathological reasons incapable of entering into such relationships.

To an ethically mature person, every human being is a human being, regardless of the group he is born into or is affiliated with. He is a human being first, and secondarily a member of this or that group.

The ethically mature person is aware of the fact that his welfare and that of his group are bound up with the welfare of the entire human race.

To attain ethical maturity it is necessary to transcend all group lines and to accept the welfare of the human race as paramount, exceeding in importance that of any of its constituent groups, including one's own. The ethically mature person repudiates the kind of allegiance that requires him to place the interest of his group above that of humanity.

The brotherhood of man has been preached for thousands of years, but the results attained thus far are disappointing. One of the reasons for this is to be found in the false assumption that one could practice brotherhood at the same time that he gave primary allegiance to a group: to a nation, race, class, religious denomination, profession, and so on.

This assumption is dangerously false. Group patriotism, in the sense of primary allegiance to a group, usually precludes an ethical transcendentalism, and is therefore itself unethical. Why is this so?

The reason is this. The group patriot finds it difficult not to share his group's ambition. What is this ambition? It is usually nothing less than that of becoming the dominant, most influential, most powerful group in its field, if not in the world.

A group tends to fall a victim to what might be termed collective egotism. The group may be a movement, a party, a class, an oligarchy, a nation, a race, a sex, a religious denomination, a profession, a labor union, a chamber of commerce, a club, and so on. However rational the individual member of a group may be toward other issues, with reference to those around which the group is organized, it is difficult or impossible for him to be rational. A militant group is made up

12

largely of individuals whose orientation toward the issues around which the group is organized is on the whole irrational.

The stigmata of collective egotism can be detected in any militant group: the delusion of superiority, moral, intellectual, political; the belief in the possession of a monopoly of political intelligence and governing ability; the cosmic phantasy of the world as destined to come under its sway; the delusion of infallibility, evidenced by a fanatical dogmatism and a fierce intolerance; an acute fear of inquiry, criticism and discussion; a ceaseless tendency to discover conspiracies against itself everywhere; a hatred of opposition that sometimes becomes insensate and breaks out in violence; an insistence that all things be patterned to conform to its ideology. Some of these items may be lacking in any given case, others may be present to a moderate degree, but every militant group is sure to exhibit at least a few of these features.

Once the fact of collective egotism is grasped, an explanation of one of the great paradoxes of group behavior becomes possible. It is paradoxical that movements which evince such solicitude for social welfare, brotherly love, culture and civilization, often contribute too little to these, and too much to the sum-total of barbarism already extant. The paradox need surprise no one. The much-talked of and little understood idealism of militant movements is in part or in whole an expression of their delusions of grandeur and messianic mission. These are an expression of love of power. Power is what the group wants first, last, and all the time. Whatever helps it attain power it terms good; whatever thwarts it in its quest it calls evil. And in collective egotism the opposition often becomes an object of insensate hatred and panicky fear; both these affects often find expression in violence.

Too close an attachment to a militant group may therefore cause the moral sense to become blunted. Everything the group does, no matter how destructive, no matter how degenerate in character, may come to seem right and proper. Everything that other and rival groups do, no matter how constructive, may come to seem wrong and immoral. The same deed is moral or immoral, depending on whether it is performed by one's own or a rival group.

It is of course true that the idealism of a group is often sincere. But of that more anon.

A social psychologist tells a story that points up group egotism in most exquisite fashion. It is the story of Hassan, the date peddler who sold his wares in an Oriental bazaar.

Daily Hassan trudged the streets with his date basket. He was but one of many date peddlers in the bazaar, but there was one thing that distinguished him from all the others. This was the peculiar way he advertised his wares. As he tramped the streets, he would cry, "My dates are larger than they are! My dates are larger than they are!"

The group is like that date peddler. All group propaganda tends to express the same motif: we are larger than we are! We are bigger than we are! We are more important, more powerful! We are at the center of the universe! Our nation is the greatest on earth. Our race is the Herrenvolk. Our class is the backbone of society. We are the more important sex. Our party possesses a genius for government. To our church has been vouchsafed the revelation. Our program is the hope of humanity. If we do not lead, the world will lapse into chaos. And so on *ad nauseam*.

It is all so very pathetic. It is a sign of a lack of a sense of proportion, of humorlessness, and of ethical immaturity. Most people value the things that make for conflict and strife, degradation and slavery. They crave power and dominion and hegemony. Acting singly, they find it difficult to attain their desires. But what they cannot obtain individually, they may obtain acting in concert. In union there is strength; united, the spiritually weak may become politically strong. The poor in spirit, when they pool their poverty, may find it easier to gain political power and economic wealth.

But if our dates are larger than they are, then the other peddlers' dates must be smaller than they are. Other and competing groups are composed of people who are less important and in ever so many respects inferior to us. They are not located at the center of the universe; they belong to its periphery, if they belong in the universe at all. If they do belong in the universe, they have been placed there for a reason so obvious that it hardly needs telling; they are meant to be ruled by our group. They are brought into being to provide our group with material to work upon, something on which to test itself, something on which to impose its hegemony. The world needs leadership. Someone must plan. Someone must make the decisions. Who is better fitted for these tasks than our group, our nation, our race, our class, our sex, our profession, our church, composed as it is of the superior people—superior morally, superior intellectually, superior in the arts of government?

All this may sound funny. It is funny, but it is also tragic, very tragic, and it is the cause of so much of the world's tragedy. And the tragedy it generates will continue to persist as long as men and women, in their ethical immaturity, continue to lay great stress on group patriotisms. Group patriotisms have in the past proved to be well-nigh fatal to the attainment of the ideal of brotherhood.

This is not just another plea for brotherhood. It is more than that. The preachers of brotherhood have always behaved as if they thought that the attainment of their ideal required nothing more than an exertion of will in the direction of democracy and love on the part of their hearers and readers. An exertion of the will in these directions is required, to be sure. But the will must also exert itself in the transcendence of group boundaries and group patriotisms. It must exert itself in the cultivation of an ethically transcendental attitude, the attitude that leads one to envisage oneself as first of all a human being, and only secondarily an American, a German, a Protestant, a Jew, a capitalist, a worker, a Negro, a white person, a man, a woman, and so on.

The question is this: shall people take their ethical obligations seriously? They cannot take them very seriously as long as they are subject to the ravages of collective egotism. That kind of spiritual illness is hostile to ethical maturation.

❀ ❀ ❀ ❀

True enough, a group is not the expression of unmitigated evil and unqualified selfishness. Its ambitions and its striving need not be entirely ignoble. It may entertain ideals of the highest kind. It may evince a desire to lift all the world to a higher plane of living. Many of the members of a group stand ready to sacrifice all, even life itself, for the ideal. All this is granted.

Within the life of the group, however, there rages a conflict, a conflict between its altruism and its egotism. The two tendencies usually effect a compromise. The latter is usually revealing. Since the group pictures itself as at the center of the universe, the chosen of the gods, with a membership made up of the superior people, it comes to conceive its destiny as messianic. Its role is to be that of savior. To it belongs the future. To it therefore belong the key positions, the seats of power, and all the associated special rights and privileges. It feels certain that without these it cannot fulfill its noble and altruistic mission. It is equally sure that once it obtains them, it will employ them for noble purposes only.

Such is the character of the compromise. But the compromise is too one-sided. The group's egotism comes out the real victor. One of the things that makes this possible is the fact that people have not yet learned that, as a general thing, ethical goals cannot be attained by unspiritual means. And when they think they are attaining ethical ends in this manner, what is really happening is that these are being replaced by goals of another than ethical character. This is exactly what happens in the life of the group. And this is one of the reasons why "successful" movements of revolution or reform often prove to be such disappointing failures.

This helps to explain why no group, however lofty its ideals, however noble its sentiments, can lead the human race onto the road to salvation. No group can take on the role of messiah. No group can save the world—every group is itself in need of salvation. It has all it can do to save itself.

Humanity cannot be saved by any group, no matter how large, no matter how important. It cannot be saved by any nation, any race, any church, any class, any party, any sex. It cannot and will not be saved by the proletariat, by the middle class, by the Anglo-Saxons, by the Catholic church, by the Protestants, by the United States, by the liberals, by the technocrats, by the psychoanalysts, by the scientists, or by the women. How can any group save humanity, when the salvation of the latter requires it to transcend group loyalties and group feelings? But such a transcendence cannot be tolerated by any group.

The case can be put this way. No group can save humanity, and this for the reason that salvation requires an end to group dominance. Group dominance and human brotherhood are mutually exclusive. But dominance is precisely what the group, openly or secretly, dreams of and longs for.

There is yet another way of putting it. The salvation of humanity must be spiritual. It must lie in a subordination of wealth and power to aims and values that are religious, ethical, aesthetic and intellectual in character. The group, dreaming of dominance, tends to place too high an evaluation on power and prestige values, and generally on economic values as well.

The lesson is clear. People must learn to outgrow their dependence on militant groups and group leaders: on parties and politicians and political wonder-workers; on revolutionists and counter-revolutionists; on labor leaders and captains of industry; and on any and all militant movements and organizations, no matter how beautiful their expressed ideals, no matter how prepossessing their programs, no matter how plausible their philosophies. They must learn to bear this in mind, that the expressed ideals, programs and philosophies of a militant movement or group serve to conceal its secret aim: to acquire and enjoy power, wealth and dominion. The problem of living together is fundamentally an ethical problem, and one of the essential elements

in its solution is an ethical transcendentalism. But the latter is something no militant group can tolerate.

This is not to be misunderstood. Men and women are not being
asked to cast off all patriotisms and to spurn all group allegiances. To
ask this is to ask the impossible. What is insisted on is this, that all
group allegiances and group patriotisms be ranked as subordinate to
an ethical transcendentalism. Such a subordination seems necessary
if people are to outgrow their national and race conflicts, their class
struggles, their imperialisms and militarisms, their collective egotisms.

❖   ❖   ❖   ❖

The thinking of a militant group invariably reveals large elements
of phantasy. The so-called ideology of a group is in large part a collective day-dream, a pseudo-philosophical, fantastic view of the cosmos. It is necessary to turn to a consideration of the cosmic phantasy.

5

THE COSMIC PHANTASY

A militant group—that is, a nation, race, religious denomination, political party, class, sex, social movement—feels it must justify itself to itself and the world. It feels it must convince itself and others that it is a chosen group, chosen of God or fate, that it is "in tune with the universe," that its hegemony, its ultimate dominance, are assured, certified, guaranteed by the very nature of things, by the very structure of the cosmos itself. The group will therefore have its "philosophers," in reality pseudo-philosophers. These are charged with the duty of formulating the "true" philosophy. Theirs is the task of "discovering" that the universe is just what the group wants it to be, and that the group's predestined fate is precisely what it would like it to be. Further, they must perform this task in a way that makes it possible to describe the finished product as truly philosophical, logical, scientific.

This is quite a task. But the procedure the pseudo-philosophers follow is not too complicated. It consists in the selection of those presuppositions and facts, and in the formulation of those definitions that will lead to and "prove" the desired conclusions. It is of course essential that the pseudo-philosopher shall not be too critical of these pre-suppositions and definitions and of the procedure itself. Such criticism, if indulged in by anyone in or out of the group, is dismissed as a sign of arrogance or prejudice or pedantry, as carping, or perhaps as subversive and immoral. Nor are the pseudo-philosophers unprepared to meet the criticism that their procedure is unscientific and irrational. They will counter the charge of being unscientific with the reply that there are some things that lie beyond the ken of science. The assertion that their "philosophy" and procedure are irrational they will meet with the announcement that they are really relying on something mightier, more penetrating than reason, namely, intuition. So there you are. It is not easy to argue with a convinced believer. Nor is it any easier to carry on a controversy with a "philosophical" apologist for a power-seeking group.

❖　❖　❖　❖

The pseudo-philosophy of a militant group can be termed a cosmic phantasy. The latter pictures the world as having been brought into

18

being for the express purpose of giving one's own group, the "my" group, something to rule, something to dominate. The world has from all time been destined to come under its sway. The cosmos is so constituted that its evolution can lead to but one result: the supremacy of the my group. The ultimate victory of the latter is inevitable. It is decreed by fate, by evolution, by the absolute, by the dialectic, or by deity itself; it is written in the stars: "The stars in their courses fight for us."

The cosmic phantasy offers drama as well as "philosophy." It visualizes the world as a battleground between the forces of good and those of evil. One's own group is of course the guardian of goodness, truth, beauty and justice, of hearth and home, of prosperity and progress. Rival groups, being composed of the wicked or the well-intentioned but misled, are a menace to all that is valuable and dear. Their dominance is or would be a social calamity of the first magnitude. Indeed, it is to the dominance of groups other than one's own that a good part, if not most, of the world's evils is to be attributed.

The cosmic phantasy thus presents a Zoroastrian aspect. The cosmos is a battlefield. The protagonists are Ahura Mazda and Ahriman, god and devil, good and evil, justice and injustice, truth and error, beauty and ugliness. But the cosmic phantasy is optimistic. The ultimate victory of Ahura Mazda, of the god, of the absolute, is assured. These are conceived as omnipotent, or at any rate as more powerful; right will therefore triumph in the end. This insures the eventual ascendency of the my group, for it is this group which has from all time been destined to undertake the guardianship of all that is worth guarding.

It goes without saying that the assumption by one's own group of a position of dominance is conceived as ushering in a new era. It might not be exactly Utopia, but it will come pretty close to it. Since the my group is the chosen of the Lord, or the absolute, or the dialectic, or whatever the ultimate principle might be, and since it is composed of the ethically, intellectually, and politically superior people, what other result can there be? And so every group fondly imagines that the day it rides into power will see a rebirth for humanity. Gone or diminished will be the old evils. There will take place a transvaluation of values. Humanity will burst its fetters; it will come up into the light.

The cosmic phantasy contains, therefore, an eschatological, a messianic element. A militant group regards itself as the messiah, the savior that the world has always been waiting for. Naturally so, for it is for its sake that the world was brought into being. The world has been existing and evolving, preparing the way for the coming of the saviour group.

One recalls here the remark made by Everett Dean Martin, to whom I am greatly indebted, in his book, *The Behavior of Crowds*, that a crowd holds that only one solution of the social problem is possible, and that one inevitable—its own.

It is significant that the group conceives its ascent into power as entailing the discomfiture, the humiliation of other and rival groups. To the victor belong the spoils. The dominance of the proletariat, in reality the dominance of the professional revolutionist, will mean the discomfiture of the capitalists. In the feminist cosmic phantasy, men are reduced to the rank of assistants to the women, who are destined to become the leaders in every field of ethical, intellectual and artistic endeavor.

                              *   *   *   *

Is it necessary to furnish proof of the correctness of this description of the thinking of the militant group? The evidence is there for all to see. One has but to read the literature of a group or listen to its speakers or talk to any of its members to perceive the outlines of its cosmic phantasy. Of particular importance is it to read, listen or talk to the pseudo-philosophers or pseudo-scientists of a group.

It seems to make no difference what kind of a group it is, provided it is militant in character. The group may be a nation, a race, a class, a sex, a political party, a profession, a religious denomination, a reform movement, a revolutionary or counter-revolutionary movement: if it is militant, it will in all likelihood have its cosmic phantasy. And the latter will always be propagated in the same uncritical, humorless fashion.

Every one of the great religions conceives itself as the specially selected vehicle of divine or cosmic truth. To it, and to it alone, has been vouchsafed the great revelation, or at any rate the chief revelation. Every one of the great religious groups therefore conceives itself as in some sense chosen. This disposes of all doubts concerning its ultimate triumph. As the vehicle of the deity, it shares something of the divine omnipotence. To it and to the deity belong the universe. There is no mistaking whom deity had in mind when it created the cosmos.

There is, however, no essential difference between the cosmic phantasy of religious groups and that of other kinds. Any militant group tends to regard itself as especially favored by deity, by the absolute, by the dialectic, by evolution, by the very structure of the universe, or by whatever else it considers the ultimate principle of things.

The world has become familiar with racial cosmic phantasies, and it has seen to what uses they can be put. It has had many an unfortunate experience with the notion of predestined national hegemony, a euphemism for imperialism. Today the world has to deal with a movement with a "philosophy" centered around an evolutionary principle known as the dialectic, conceived as a principle of progress by conflict. The very idea of conflict is dear to the heart of every militant group. The dialectical progression is held pointed to the realization of the classless society. This has a democratic sound, but there is a qualification. The dialectic, it seems, has been thoughtful enough so to arrange matters as to make the "temporary" dominance of the proletariat a requisite for the realization of the democratic ideal. A cosmic phantasy always pictures the ultimate cosmic principle, be it what it may, as exhibiting this kind of thoughtfulness in its relation to the power-seeking group.

Each sex has its cosmic phantasy. There are many men and women who are certain that the position and function of their sex in the cosmic economy mark it out for special favors. Masculinist and feminist cosmic phantasies usually incorporate a pseudo-biology, a pseudo-psychology and a pseudo-sociology. Masculinist and feminist are certain that nature has all along "meant" that his (or her) sex shall rule. The procedure by which what nature "means" is "established" consists of the selection of those biological, psychological and sociological facts, fancied or real, which support the conclusion one desires to reach. This procedure, it must be repeated, is standard in all cosmic phantasy formation. The creator of a cosmic phantasy begins with a conclusion. He knows what he wants to "prove." He selects those assumptions and those facts, and he formulates those definitions of his terms which lead to the desired destination. The whole procedure constitutes a piece of question-begging. Prime requisites for success in cosmic phantasy building are a feeble capacity for self-criticism and a lack of a sense of humor.

The cosmic phantasy often comes dressed in scientific garb. There may be impressive arrays of graphs and statistics, and copious selections of scientific facts, real and alleged. But it is all a pose. A true scientist does not select his facts with an eye to the establishment of a preconceived conclusion. He does not begin with a conclusion that is going to be "proved" at all costs, even at the cost of truth and logic. He does not dismiss or suppress the criticism of his presuppositions as pedantic, or carping, or subversive, or immoral. He does not conceive it to be his function as a scientist to aid any militant group in its quest for power, or to weave a cosmic phantasy for it. He does not number mythopoesis among the duties of a scientist.

*   *   *   *

Psychologists have long ago repudiated the intellectualism that depicts the personality as predominately rational. The modern psychologist does not explain human behavior as a function of reason. Reason is there, to be sure, and the more psychologically mature the personality, the more of it there is. Reason plays a role, but so do other elements, and that of the latter is often prepotent. Yet in spite of what psychologists are saying, popular opinion persists in clinging to an outmoded intellectualism. And so a conflict between militant groups is often described as one between ideologies, or between rival philosophies.

A conflict between two militant groups is a good deal more than that. It is a conflict between power-lusting, power-seeking crowds. Further, their ideologies or philosophies will upon close examination be too often found to be neither ideologies nor philosophies, but pseudo-philosophies, cosmic phantasies, delusional systems.

The popular picture of two rival groups discussing, debating and weighing philosophies and ideologies is unrealistic. That discussion and debate take place is undeniable. The picture misleads, however, in its suggestion of two militant groups, composed of prepotently rational and truth-loving folk, with minds that are delightfully open, objectively weighing rival philosophies.

A conflict between militant groups is an emotional debauch. One has but to watch an election campaign to be convinced of that. The atmosphere of group conflict is hostile to rational procedure. Everything is done to arouse and intensify feeling, with radio, television, press and platform taking the lead. The sort of thinking that goes on under such circumstances is, properly speaking, not thinking, but a species of dreaming. The dream is that of one's group as superior, superior in this, superior in that, superior in so many respects to the rival group, if not to all groups. And when the dream goes on to depict the world as having been brought into being in order that it shall come under the sway of one's own group, when evolution is described as leading inexorably to the dominance of the my group, then the dream has taken on the proportions of a cosmic phantasy.

*   *   *   *

The cosmic phantasy is blasphemy. It is nothing short of blasphemy for a group to think itself the favorite of God, or the absolute, or whatever else the ultimate may be termed. The ultimate, it may be presumed, has no favorite group. It has no favorite nation, or race, or class, or party, or sex. It does not even have a favorite church. Those who think it has a pet group subsist on the level of the Sunday School pupil who wanted to know whether God is a Methodist. It is safe to assume that the ultimate, whatever it may be, is not Methodist. Neither is it Baptist, or Roman Catholic, or Jewish, or Buddhist. Nor is it American, Russian, German, Caucasian, Negro or Malay. Nor is it radical, conservative or liberal. It is not a member of the working class, the middle class, or the capitalist class. It is neither feminist nor masculinist. The ultimate is not a joiner. It follows no party line. A militant group is never more presumptuous than when it proclaims to the world, "God is with us." This is blasphemy indeed.

A group that esteems itself the favorite of God or the ultimate is not merely presumptuous. It is, or can be, dangerous. If its deeds express the will of the ultimate, then everything it does, no matter how destructive, no matter how degenerate, is conceived as right and proper. If its doctrines are received from the ultimate itself, they must be infallibly true. Dissenting doctrines must therefore be false. Thus does a group acquire a blunted sense for truth and morals. Thus does a group imprison itself in a phantasy.

❁   ❁   ❁   ❁

In order to step out of a cosmic phantasy and make contact with the real world, it is necessary to cultivate an intellectual as well as an ethical transcendentalism. The latter has already received consideration. It is necessary to go on to an examination of intellectual transcendentalism.

6

BEYOND "ISMS" TO REASON

Intellectual transcendentalism requires an escape from and an ascent above the lines separating schools of thought. A plea for such a transcendentalism should not be mistaken for just another call for an impartial pursuit of truth. It is that, but it is also more than that.

Men and women have for no one knows how many centuries been called upon impartially to pursue the truth. The plea has never been very effectual. Partisanship is intense even among philosophers and scientists. One of the reasons for this is the fact that it has been supposed that one could be an adherent to a school of thought and yet be a lover of truth. The supposition is a dangerous one. Attachment, or at any rate too close an attachment to a school of thought may be well-nigh fatal to such a love.

Consider the ways of a school of thought. What is such a school? Ideologically speaking, a school of thought—to be spoken of as school hereafter—consists of a number of persons who subscribe to a given, more or less integrated system of ideas. It is composed of persons who share a creed, a body of doctrines, a viewpoint, an orientation. It is made up of people who find each other ideologically agreeable, and who are therefore inclined to think well of each other. Every school tends to consider itself as made up of the right-minded people.

Psychologically speaking, a school may constitute what social psychologists used to call a crowd. (Chapters 4 and 5 describe crowd behavior.) Many, perhaps all, schools are crowds. A militant school is certainly a crowd. It is bent on conducting ideological warfare. It is set for attack and girded for defense. It opposes and it expects to be opposed. Such a school is the expression of the competitive way of life on the intellectual level.

A school constantly propagates what it no doubt believes to be truth. It is convinced that it disseminates the truth, and nothing but the truth. At first glance, a school appears to be made up of people who are urged on by the purest devotion to the truth. But there is more than meets the eye. It appears that the truth is something that has been vouchsafed to a select group—one's own group. The truth is something uniquely located in one's platform or creed or body of doctrines. Further, one's own group has something of a monopoly, not only of the truth, but of the lovers of truth, or at least the clear-eyed lovers of truth. It is not so with other schools. These are made up of people who are not quite so clear-eyed, when they are not self-deluded fools, or even obscurantists and liars. The platforms, creeds and statements of doctrine put out by other schools are therefore dim adumbrations of the truth, when they are not compounded of errors, falsehoods and plain lies.

It is always the other schools that exhibit these vices. One's own school is always different. How fortunate that this is so! What a good thing it is that one's own crowd should be made up of the right-minded, the clear-eyed, the intelligent people!

A school can be constituted by any kind of group. It may be a group subscribing to a philosophy, or a scientific doctrine, or a fashion in art. It may be a religious group, a social movement, a cult or the followers of a fad. It may be a nation, a race, a class, a sex, a party, a profession, a trade union. It is any group proclaiming an "ism."

There seems to be little doubt that affiliation with a school imposes serious handicaps on the genuine seeker after truth. The handicaps are both psychological and logical. The psychological handicaps are only too evident. First there is a kind of social pressure. A member of a school knows that all the other members expect him to remain "loyal." He is expected to remain loyal, not to truth, but to the school. He is therefore expected constantly to recite the articles of the creed. If he is a scientist or a philosopher, his researches and his thinking are looked to for "confirmation" of the validity of the creed and the correctness of the party line. Deviation from the latter is not held to be prompted by devotion to truth; it is simply a case of treachery. Deviation is heresy, and where people speak in terms of orthodoxy and heresy, one may be reasonably certain that they are exhibiting little concern for truth, and a great deal for ideological good form.

One of the severest of all handicaps imposed by a school is the almost compulsive urge to rationalize. As it manifests itself in school thinking, rationalization is ratiocination in which the demands of truth and logic are subordinated to the need for the justification of the school's urge for self-perpetuation and prestige and power. In ration-alization, the psychological takes precedence over the logical. The creed must justify; whether it edifies may or may not be so important. A school of thought is an institution, with more or less fixity and rigidity. It resists change, it dreads annihilation, and it dreams of expansion. It always feels itself under a constraint to offer good and sufficient reasons for its perpetuation and for the acquisition of influ-ence and power. Now truth cannot be depended upon always to fur-nish such good and sufficient reasons. Truth is unsafe. It is an unpredictable quality. There is no telling in advance what forms it will take, what its content will be. But rationalization can be controlled. Rationalizations can always be pointed toward the right conclusions.

The urge to rationalize has individual as well as social roots. Often, when one has taken up a position, it tends to exhibit a disconcerting tendency. It insists on being accepted as an integral part of one's self, like one's muscles or one's emotions. It then becomes difficult to repudiate, or even to modify the position; it comes to seem too much like a repudiation or modification of one's self. To part with a position to which one has for a long time adhered may come to feel like parting with something that has become hallowed by intimate association with one's personality.

So much for the psychological handicaps. What about the logical handicaps? They are just as serious.

A school of thought, as has been noted, is not wholly open to the demands of truth and logic. It exhibits emotional preferences. The latter find expression in the choice of presuppositions for its thinking. The presuppositions are partial, one-sided in character. Some one aspect of existence, of the universe, or of the field or object of inquiry is seized upon and made the focus of special treatment and attention. The treatment takes the form of a magnification of the chosen aspect and of its role and importance. The dependence of all the other aspects on the one selected is emphasized and high-lighted; its dependence on them is minimized or even denied. Or these other aspects may be depicted as mere appendages or expressions or forms of the preferred aspect. The chosen aspect is thus favored with a position of primacy, basicality, fundamentality, centrality—a position that may or may not stand rational inspection. In extreme cases, the very existence of all aspects other than the one selected may be denied, thus establishing a false monism and mistaking the part for the whole.

The preconceptions of a school, then, are built around something described as basic, fundamental, central, primary, or something that is offered as the sole reality. Those who subscribe to a school therefore consider themselves as occupying a special position in society; they see themselves as fated to play a more than ordinary role in the shaping of the future.

Such is the thinking that takes place when presuppositions express temperamental preferences or when they are chosen with a view to the conclusions it is desired to arrive at. Such presuppositions conceal important aspects of reality; they exclude whatever they cannot assimilate, and thus the conclusions come to seem confirmed. The thought of a school is as a rule little more than the eduction of the desired conclusions from the presuppositions, the eduction being facilitated by suitable definitions of terms and accompanied by an impressive array of facts, real or alleged, all properly selected. The thought of a school is therefore likely to be a monumental piece of question-begging. Often there is a great show of "self-criticism," but the standards employed are carefully selected with a view to the preservation of whatever it is desired to preserve.

It is of course not to be denied that a certain amount of honest, genuine, valid, realistic thinking does go on within the precincts of a school. But it is only too evident that the thinking of a school is in greater or lesser part a species of day-dreaming. The dream state, as has already been seen, is revealed by its Zoroastrian pattern: the conflict between one's own group and the others is one between God and the devil, between Ahura-Mazda and Ahriman, between good and evil. One's own group, of course, represents God. It champions goodness and truth; the other crowds, falsehood and evil.

This sort of dreaming issues in a distorted and over-simplified view of reality. The over-simplification operates to impoverish both action and thought by the narrowing of alternatives to two—the either-or fallacy. It comes to be taken for granted that choice is limited to two extremes: our goodness or their evil, our truth or their error: fascism or communism, socialism or capitalism, authoritarianism or license, dictatorial planning or unplanned chaos, individualism or statism, inner spiritual change or outer environmental alteration, gynocracy or androcracy, atheism or theism, idealism or materialism, monism or pluralism, and so on, and so on. When this sort of thinking goes to extremes the only choice it can offer is one between two equally destructive alternatives. The school that offers such a choice will of course be blind to the destructive character of the alternative it favors. Its rationalizations will make sure of that.

Among the most abhorrent of "isms" is specialism. Too often does specialism lead to the kind of simplism which asserts that *the* key to the understanding of the universe or life or history or the social problem or what not, lies in mathematics, or physics, or chemistry, or biology, or psychology, or economics, or political science, or religion, or diet, or glands, or heredity, or the Oedipus or some other complex, or the racial subconscious, or any one of a host of other things. This is bad enough, but specialism becomes even more of a menace when it becomes messianic. The salvation of the world then becomes something to be left to the eugenists, or the endocrinologists, or the economists, or the psychologists, or the engineers, or the social planners, or the teachers, and so on.

❋   ❋   ❋   ❋

It is clear, then, that too close an attachment to a school of thought blunts the sense for truth. Truth becomes whatever the party line asserts it is, be its assertions ever so absurd, or even contradictory. Error becomes anything condemned by the party line. The words *truth* and *error* are thus deprived of their usual and accepted meanings.

Too close an attachment to a school of thought imposes severe limitations on intellectual endeavor. To such endeavor the spirit of the schools is too often hostile; it may sometimes be fatal. The spirit of the schools is the spirit of competition and strife, of controversy and contention, of argument and debate, of conflict and war, with victory, prestige, and perhaps wealth and power, rather than truth, the prize. In justification of this spirit it is often asserted that in debate one-sidedness meets one-sidedness, the two cancel each other out, and truth issues the winner. This is not the case. One-sidedness and one-sidedness do not add up to truth. When one-sidedness meets one-sidedness, there are two perversions where there was but one before. The result may be not less, but more confusion. Certain it is that the close of a debate usually finds debaters, hearers and readers occupying the same positions they started out with, and with everyone more than ever impressed by his opponent's remarkable obtuseness.

Truth is not to be gotten at by pitting perversion against perversion, but by outgrowing and abandoning perversion altogether. Those who so much as strive to achieve this are taking a step toward intellectual maturity. On the mature level there are no "isms." There is only the distinction between the true and the untrue, or between the most acceptable hypothesis or theory and theories and hypotheses not so acceptable. But the criteria of truth and acceptability are here held to be independent of all considerations of school affiliation, power, prestige, personal interest and group pressure. The line between the true and that not established as true is seen to be not at all conterminous with any party line.

This is not a plea for mere tolerance. The merely tolerant attitude looks down on all dissentient doctrines as false, to be confuted by argument rather than suppressed. A more mature attitude, while certainly tolerant, holds that all doctrines, including one's own, are to be subjected to the tests of reason and scientific analysis.

As in the case of ethical transcendentalism, this proposal for an intellectual transcendentalism will no doubt meet with the objection that it is an ideal impossible of attainment. There is a good deal of force in this criticism. No one can help belonging to schools of thought. No one can outgrow them completely. In fact, to avoid all affiliation with any, one would have to stop thinking.

But no one is being asked to stop thinking. The position outlined here calls for more people to think, to do more thinking, and to do more thinking of the highest order. One cannot avoid belonging to schools of thought; that is true. But one can do more. One can learn to take the schools, his own included, less seriously. One can learn to regard the demands of truth and reason as prior to those of any school. One can learn to see that the truth is wider than any school; no school can possibly contain all of it. Further, truth never strings itself out along a party line.

This is a plea for the taking of one's intellectual obligations seriously. Taking one's intellectual obligations seriously means the espousal of intellectual transcendentalism. It means going beyond a rhetorical devotion to truth. A genuine devotion involves, or should involve, a frank and full acceptance of reason and scientific method. Such an acceptance means using reason and science in the evaluation, not only of the other fellow's, but one's own ideas as well. It means subjecting to rational examination the presuppositions of one's own, as well as of other sets of doctrine, in an endeavor to expose one-sidedness, emotional preferences and falsehoods.

It also means another thing. It means the frank acceptance of the limitations of the human mind. The universe being what it is, and the human mind being what it is, it appears to be true that certainty of knowledge is rarely attainable. The best that can usually be hoped for is knowledge possessed of a fairly high degree of probability. This means there is no choice but to be content with ideas and systems of ideas that are subject to change. Hence one must once and for all outgrow the habit of swearing permanent allegiance to this or that system of ideas. This means an end to dogma. This is nothing to be sorry about, for a dogma is after all nothing but a hypothesis or theory vested in a delusive sense of certitude. An indoctrinated idea, an idea that has been uncritically received and made into a permanent mental fixture, an idea that is emotionally charged, all become or tend to become dogmas.

Reason and scientific method are here offered as instruments by means of which it is possible to win liberation from the mind-enslaving, mind-distorting, mind-stunting influence of "isms" and schools of thought. They are offered as the means by which men and women can go farther on the road to intellectual maturity.

✻   ✻   ✻   ✻

Liberation from "isms," doctrines, creeds and party lines might conceivably mean the end of political parties and party government. It might mean the entrance of the politician into the category of extinct animals. It might involve the replacement of the politician by trained legislative and administrative experts, constantly working together with scientists and critically responsive to their advice. It might also involve the replacement of the large, cumbersome bicameral legislature, congress or parliament by a relatively small, compact unicameral council.

All of these changes should be most welcome. A political party, as was pointed out in a preceding chapter, is a creature motivated by collective egotism. The egotism is manifested among other things in a phantasy-system labelled ideology, creed, dogma, doctrine and party line. The nature of this phantasy-system has already been described in the chapter on the cosmic phantasy.

It is of course undeniable that a party is not all egotism, phantasy and love of power. Many a party adherent is sincere and many a truth may be found in a party manifesto and party platform. But this does not change the over-all picture. All things considered, a political party is an irrational creature, with a craving for power, and little or no regard for truth, logic and scientific process. It prefers propaganda to education, intellectual conformity to intellectual creativity, stereotyped thinking to critical analysis. True, it believes in criticism—when directed against other parties. It prefers not to be a target for any criticism, whether from within or without.

It is time to dispense with the false notion that an election campaign has educational value. Perhaps it has, for a few. But an election campaign is not an educational device; it is an emotional debauch. Party propaganda and campaign speeches are designed to make the masses more susceptible to manipulation; they are not calculated to spur voters to independent thinking or to facilitate intellectual maturation.

It is not proposed to abolish elections; it is proposed to alter the spirit in which they are conducted, to lift them to a more mature level. Given a governmental or non-governmental organization staffed by trained legislative and administrative experts, guided by scientific counsellors, some of the elections would deal, not with candidates, but with issues. They would be referenda, with the electoral body making its selection from the alternatives put before it by the voters themselves or by legislatures and administrative agencies.

The ultimate result of all this might be the taking of government out of politics, in the pejorative sense of the term. At the very least it might go far toward lifting the citizen a notch or two above the immature level occupied by the party system, with its stifling of reason and logical and scientific process and its cultivation of empty, deceptive rhetoric and stereotyped and slogan thinking. Governments might find themselves able to grapple somewhat more realistically with the problems they are called upon to solve.

The combination of trained administrator and scientific counsellor may be found a feasible one for non-governmental bodies. Consumer and producer cooperatives, labor unions, professional associations, fraternal orders and business organizations may use it; some of them have indeed done so to a limited degree. This would constitute an experiment of the greatest importance, for it is non-governmental cooperative self-aid that people must learn to have increasing resort to if they are to steer clear of the destructive effects of predatory individualism on the one hand, and governmental tyranny on the other.

The proposal to equip governmental and non-governmental agencies with scientific counsel is sure to meet with objections. Among the most strenuous objectors will be many of the social scientists themselves. They plead that the social and allied sciences do not as yet possess a fund of knowledge great enough to permit them to function in the manner proposed. But those who speak in this fashion fail to grasp the issue. The issue is not that of replacing less knowledge by more; rather is it that of replacing irrationalism, phantasy and stereotyped thinking by rational and objective attitudes and procedures. What the scientist and the scientifically trained administrator and legislator must contribute is a new spirit, a new attitude, a willingness to submit to objective, rational, scientific procedures. This is what is sorely needed—not more knowledge primarily, but a new spirit.

❀   ❀   ❀   ❀

The position outlined in this chapter will perhaps be charged with inconsistency. Some may say another "ism" is being offered. Some may say another school of thought is being proposed.

Intellectual transcendentalism is not just another "ism," not just another school of thought. If it ever gains any followers it will undoubtedly become a school of thought. But it will be a school dedicated to the proposition that the truth is too large to be contained within the boundaries of any school; that the truth does not follow a party line; that it does not come wrapped in dogma; that all ideas and systems of ideas, including its own, are subject to criticism, correction, change and rejection. It will be a school of thought, but it will be more than that; it will be a way of transcending schools of thought.

*   *   *   *

To pursue truth and pursue it truly is to pursue it wholly. To want truth is to want to know reality, reality as it really is. To select a portion of reality, a segment of the truth, and to fill in the remainder with phantasms, dreams and falsehoods is to evince a desire for something other than truth. The desire is to ensconce oneself in a fantasy, and whatever truth is received is accepted on the basis of its capacity for being assimilated into the fantasy.

To pursue truth, then, is to open oneself to the whole, to all things, to the cosmos itself. A biased approach signifies the subordination of reason, and therefore of reality, to the demands of fantasy. Bias, if it deigns to look upon reality at all, selects a segment thereof, and suppresses the rest. It then childishly convinces itself that the suppressed remainder really has no existence at all. It acts as if it thought that to deny the existence of anything were equivalent to its annihilation. Bias is therefore a kind of dreaming, a species of fantasy. The biased person lives in an unreal world. It is a world ruled by the laws of magic. Nothing exists therein except that upon which one sets the seal of approval. One recalls here Alfred Adler's assertion that the neurotic wishes to be godlike—in the sense of possessing omnipotence. Bias is not ill health, but it is not very far from it. The sick mind is closed to the whole. It will have no truck with universality and wholeness. It constructs its own world, and it admits into that world, in addition to fictions, those segments of the real that promise to create no disturbance. The affinity of bias and mental illness is evident.

In the last two or three decades the social scientists have been gaining favor. An increasingly large number of people are looking to them to rescue the world from its present impasse. Unfortunately, however, many envisage the social sciences as a kind of magic that can be relied upon to bring about an easy and effortless salvation. Too many of us are searching for push-button solutions.

7

PUSH-BUTTON SOLUTIONS

Again and again one hears expressed the wish that the social sciences could discover or formulate a law which in fundamentality and importance should be to human affairs what relativity and the quantum theory are to physics, natural selection to biology, the theory of the unconscious to psychology. Those who give expression to this wish usually go on to assert that such a law might furnish the key to the solution of the world's social, economic and political problems. It might very well, they think, be the means of leading the world out of its present crisis. And so they petition the social scientists to redouble their efforts, to work hard and try to bring forth this much-desired law.

One may feel justified in the suspicion that people who talk in this fashion are guilty of evasion. One may also be equally justified in supposing them to be believers in magic. They look to science to save them, to solve their problems for them, to lead them out of a crisis, and all without an expenditure of a certain kind of effort on their part. They want a push-button solution of their problems.

What could the social sciences possibly discover that would make unnecessary the practice of magnanimity, sympathy, democracy, justice and rationality? What scientific law could release people from the necessity and obligation of effecting an inner transformation? What scientific formula could, without any effort on their part, heal them, make them whole, raise them to a higher level of being, compel them to grow into greater maturity? These are the things that are required for the resolution of society's problems. The social sciences are not likely to discover them to be undesirable or unnecessary. They are not likely to discover any substitutes for them.

It will probably be argued that what the social sciences might do is to describe the conditions under which the inner transformation might best take place, the conditions and circumstances under which the ethical life and the life of reason may best flourish. This is indeed one of the things the social sciences should do and what they might do. But it must not be forgotten that the findings of the sciences cannot receive application except where there exists the will to apply them. Men and women will not establish conditions favorable to ethical and intellectual growth unless they are sufficiently ethical and intellectual to want to grow in these directions. There is no magic in science. It can in no way make people ethical and rational against their will. That is not its function. An entirely immoral and irrational person would not want to be transformed, and he might not be interested in knowing what the social sciences could do about it.

Another consideration must detain us here. Suppose the social sciences should announce the desired fundamental discovery or law. How would it be received? How have new ideas been received in the past? If history is at all a guide, it is safe to say that the new and fundamental discovery or law would in all likelihood meet with great and violent opposition. This would certainly be the case if the discovery or law constituted a threat to vested interests of any kind whatsoever. It would most certainly be the case if it ran counter to cherished habits of thought and conduct. It would probably be denounced and perhaps suppressed as false, subversive and immoral. The social scientists would have quite a task on their hands attempting to gain it a hearing. In so doing they would probably become objects of persecution. In short, they would most likely meet the fate of those who espouse new ideas. They would probably meet the fate of all who challenge the validity of accepted notions.

Nothing that is being said here should be interpreted as a depreciation of the social sciences or of the importance and value of any discovery they might make or any law they might formulate. The social sciences are needed, and never more so than today. But it is one thing to apply the social sciences to the solution of social problems, and it is quite another thing to look to them to save people the trouble of effecting an inner transformation and of growing into maturity.

There can be no push-button solution of the world's problems.

        *   *   *   *

Much the same answer can be given to those who look to a new philosophy to emerge and conquer the world and save it from destruction. That a new philosophy is needed is indeed true, and this book is itself a humble contribution thereto. A new philosophy, espousing an ethical and intellectual transcendentalism and a democratic and cooperative society, is indeed called for. But the new philosophy must also be an old philosophy, old in the sense that it receive and accept the truths borne by the philosophies of the past and present. This means that the new philosophy will put first things first, and central things in the center. It will assert the primacy of religious, ethical, aesthetic and intellectual values. It will affirm the necessity of employing ethical means for the realization of ethical aims. It will lay heavy stress on the necessity for individual and social transformation. It will never cease to expound the virtues of sympathy, magnanimity, cooperation, democracy, rationality, and scientific method. All this and more will it share with the old philosophies.

A new philosophy would conceivably have some new truths to propound. But many of its truths would be old, truths that are already known to many of us. This being the case, we can proceed to apply these old truths without waiting for the new philosophy to come and urge us to. There is no need to wait. We know the truths in question, and we are acutely aware of the urgent need to apply them, and apply them at once, here and now. We would be losing precious time waiting for a new philosophy to come and remind us that the old truths are still true. We do not need such reminders. Our duty is clear.

       ✿   ✿   ✿   ✿

There are things to be done and to be done right now, things that can be done without waiting for a new philosophy or a fundamental discovery by the social sciences. There is danger in such waiting. The danger lies in the temptation to mark time until the desired philosophy arrives, or until the social sciences announce the longed-for discovery. Such a wait may become endless. The social sciences may make many discoveries and none of them may look like the expected fundamental formulation. As for philosophy, the possibility is that there will be, not one, but many new philosophies, all of them inadequate, as philosophies cannot help being. None may appear to be the saving philosophy.

Good sense demands that people use what they have. The need is urgent and they must fall back on the truths they already possess. And if these be put to work, one of the by-products may very well be a new philosophy or a fundamental discovery by the social sciences.

       ✿   ✿   ✿   ✿

If there can be no such thing as a push-button solution of social problems, neither can there be any such thing as a solution by magic, be it the magic of a leader or wonder-working individual, or the magic of a powerful, dominant or dominance-seeking, wonder-working group. It is therefore useless to wait for a messiah. Such a wait entails a tragic waste of time, for the kind of salvation the world needs cannot be mediated by any individual, no matter how powerful, nor by any group, no matter how large, no matter how dominant.

8

TWO KINDS OF MESSIAHS

There are two kinds of messiahs: individual and collective. The individual kind is well-known. He is the great man, the savior, the buddha, the avatar, the deity incarnate whose coming will end an old era and usher in a new one. He will take upon himself the burdens of the world, he will relieve it of its sorrow, he will dispense with its problems. This conception of the messiah is monistic.

But there is another type of messiah—the collective or pluralistic messiah. It may well be called the group messiah. The popular conception of it is that it is influential and powerful or likely to acquire influence and power in the near future. It is envisaged as bringing all humanity under its sway; it will lead the world into a new era. It will work wonders. It will take upon itself the burdens of the world, it will have the answers to all questions, it will possess the key to all problems. All that the world need do to be saved is to submit to its benign rule.

There has perhaps never been a group of any influence which has not been looked upon as a collective messiah in effect. Nations, races, religious groups, classes, sexes, professions, political parties, reform, revolutionary and counter-revolutionary movements have all been looked to for salvation by a world that has never outgrown an immature, external view thereof.

Instance this modern world. An up to date list of collective messiahs, potential and current, would have to include the United States, the British Empire, Germany, France, Russia, the Anglo-Saxons, the Teutons, the Slavs, Christianity, Judaism, socialism, communism, anarchism, fascism, the scientists, the technocrats, the middle class, the proletariat, big business, the psychoanalysts, the women. Many others could be added. There will continue to be more as long as people do not or will not learn that salvation is not a task that any one or any thing can perform for another or other persons.

The belief in messiahs, individual or collective, is a belief in magic. It represents a wish for effortless salvation. It will achieve the better world, the superior society, the new morality without requiring any arduous and painful effort. Somehow and in some way the messiah will change things for the better. He or it will chart a path, he or it will lead the way, and all one will have to do is simply accept the new dispensation.

As might be expected, power-seeking, influence-craving groups have always done their utmost to keep the belief in collective messiahs and their magic alive. Many a group has indeed promoted itself as the long-expected, long-awaited messiah.

Objection will made that religious groups have always upheld an inner, as against an external view of salvation, that they have always stressed the need for inner change, the taking off of the old man and the putting on of the new, the personal rebirth. This is indeed true. However, it is also true that religious groups have leaned too heavily on rite and ritual; they have too greatly encouraged a preoccupation with symbols and ceremonials. Institutionalized religion has been to a very great extent formalized, mechanized religion. It has been religion dominated by priest, rather than mystic, saint and prophet. The latter have too often been shoved aside, when they have not been made the objects of persecution.

Certain it is, however, that a militant, power-hunting group always finds it to its interest to foster an external view of salvation. It promises the world a facile solution of all its problems, if only the world would be docile enough to put itself under its sway.

The world finds it difficult to learn that no one person, no matter how great, and no group, no matter how large, no matter how powerful, no matter how influential, can bring it salvation. They cannot bring it to even one person. All the people, all the groups in the world cannot effect a transformation within me, unless I will it. Such a transformation will involve the reformation of my behavior pattern, but that is a task that only I can undertake to perform. No one can undertake to perform it for me, for in order to do so he would have to become physically identical with me. No group, be it ever so large, can undertake it for me, for it too would have to become physically identical with me. Hence neither I nor any one else can be saved by another, or by the Anglo-Saxons, the proletariat, the communists, the engineers, the scientists, or the women.

The truth of this is attested to by modern psychiatry. Psychiatric therapy, be its technique what it may, involves a process of re-education. The latter requires the patient to take hold of himself, acquire a measure of self-control, and recast his behavior-pattern. He must learn to respond to the world in new and more adequate ways; he must establish new habits; he must lift himself to a higher level of being. All these things he must do for himself; the psychiatrist cannot do them for him. When psychiatry fails, it is often because the patient looks upon it as a kind of magic, and upon the psychiatrist as a magician. This kind of patient wants an effortless cure. He wants the psychiatrist to do all the work. But neither for the individual nor the world is there such a thing as an effortless cure. There is no effortless salvation.

This is not to assert that the external world can play no role in personal salvation. That world can stimulate, it can urge, it can facilitate, it can bring pressure, it can punish and reward, it can effect environmental changes that would make an inner transformation desirable. But none of these are equivalent to such a transformation. In the last analysis, this has to be willed. And no one can will it except the self. No one but the self can save itself. Every self has its own messiah residing within it. And to the self that has saved itself, to the self that has transfigured itself, the messiah has appeared.

❊   ❊   ❊   ❊

It will be contended that while it is indeed true that a dominant group cannot bring about an inner transformation in any person, it could nevertheless effect the kind of salvation the world is right now in need of. Among the things the world is right now in need of are the abolition of war, the control of atomic power, the furtherance of democracy and freedom, the elimination of racial and religious tensions, the limitation of population growth, and the establishment of a cooperative economic order. These are the world's most urgent, or among its most urgent needs. It would be fine, it is averred, if some powerful group could take hold and govern long enough to effect these reforms and bring the present crisis to an end.

Maybe it would be fine—for some people. It would not be fine for some people, myself included. I do not want any group to bring me a better world on a golden platter. I want no group to save this world for me. I want neither the Christians nor the Anglo-Saxons nor the working class nor the middle class nor the scientists nor the women nor anybody else to serve me in that way.

It is part of my definition of a better world that it is one that I help build. If I have no part in building it, it is not the kind of world I want to live in. In such a world I would feel like a guest—not a citizen. I have no desire to be a guest. I insist on being a citizen. I insist on making my special and unique contribution to the solution of the problems of my time. I insist that if there is to be a better world, it should be in some small part my own creation. I would not feel at home in any other kind of world. I therefore reject all collective messiahs and their "superior" worlds. I refuse to bow to them.

*   *   *   *

Millions of men and women have for long sought the transformation of the world through messianic radicalism. This movement has failed. It has not saved the world. It is itself badly in need of salvation. Instead of lifting the world to a higher level, it has yielded to the world and descended to its level. It thinks it is conquering the world; in reality it has been conquered by the world. Its failure is directly traceable to its ethical immaturity.

9

THE ETHICAL IMMATURITY OF MODERN RADICALISM

One of the greatest and most pathetic failures of history is that of modern radicalism.

This term—modern radicalism—is used here to cover the socialist, communist, anarchist and syndicalist movements of the nineteenth and twentieth centuries. It constitutes one of the most futile, one of the most tragic phenomena of all time. Modern radicalism has been a failure from the moment of its inception and it is doomed to failure even where it is most successful. The reason for this lies in the fact that modern radicalism is ethically immature.

Radicals have been sadly lacking in ethical and psychological insight. Of the profounder aspects of human nature they know nothing. How can they know? In a pathetic attempt at being scientific, they have swallowed materialism and determinism hook, line and sinker, too often without anything more than a hazy notion of the real status of these concepts. As a rule, they do not begin to suspect that these concepts, when unqualified, are not the established results of scientific research; they are metaphysical presuppositions that many scientists find it useful to employ. By way of keeping up the scientific pretense, radicals have gone in for economics, political science and sociology on a big scale. How much of the science of the radicals is genuine, and how much myth and rationalization, is a question. But all of this has issued in a superficial and distorted view of the human personality. The latter has come to be viewed by the radicals as a mechanism, its behavior mechanically determined by the social system it is born into and lives under. The personality is a completely determined affair, and from a scientific standpoint, as the radicals conceive it, its status in the universe is exactly the same as that of a stone, a cloud, a planet, an electron, an amoeba, or a plant.

Such a determinism cannot help but misconceive the social problem. From its standpoint, the kind of human being that prophets, saints and philosophers have yearned for will come into being if and when there is established the sort of social system that can "produce" him. Such a system will grind out such beings as a meat chopper grinds out meat.

The radical puts the cart before the horse. He overlooks a very important fact. It is this, that no social institution can be changed in the slightest particular unless there is present the will to change. There can be no change except as the spirit changes. The ethical change must come first.

Radicalism has misconceived the problem in that it has all along assumed that institutional change must come first. But how is that to be brought about? The radical answer is that this would be caused by social, economic and political forces. What are social, economic and political forces? It is at this point that radical thought becomes confusion worse confounded. Its conception of social forces and institutions is abstract, impersonal and mechanical. Radical literature fairly reeks with such terms as capitalism, the state, industry, finance, the church, the family, the school, the law, civilization, culture, and so on. These are discussed as if they were vast overarching affairs, existing in some upper realm, over and above human beings, and mechanically determining the behavior of these humans down below. The radical has a disdain for the humbler view of social forces which defines them as human beings, human needs, human wills acting in concert or opposition, and which sees social institutions as the customary, persistent ways in which human beings orient themselves with reference to each other. There are no forces other than human beings which can be depended upon to effect institutional changes. Hence, when radicals speak of institutional change as coming first, they betray their confusion and their feeble grasp of social and psychological realities.

The impersonal approach is apparent in the phrase *economic determinism,* and the statement that the means of production and distribution determine the culture of a time and place. A change in the former determines a change in the latter. The role played by human beings seems to be purely mechanical. They appear to be merely mechanical transmitters of the effect.

(One must mention another bad habit that radicals have. When they deign to speak of human beings, it is generally in terms of masses and classes. The result is abominable. A class is conceived as if all its members were as much alike as peas in a pod. A differential individual psychology is thus rendered impossible. Under such circumstances, it is asking too much to expect the radical to exhibit any but the feeblest insight into human nature.)

In fairness to radicalism, two concessions must be made. It must be conceded that its practice is often better than its theory. In practice, radicals do admit that ethical change comes first. Their leaders and propagandists do endeavor to influence and alter the attitudes, the spirit, the wills of those they address. They have no other recourse. The institution-change-first theory is obviously impracticable.

It will of course be conceded that the society he is born into and lives in does mold the individual. A competitive, exploitative, authoritarian society may find expression in one type of personality, a democratic, cooperative, free society in another and maturer. I insist only that the relation between the individual and his society is not unilateral, but reciprocal. It is just as true that the institutions of a people express its spirit, as it is that the spirit of a people is an expression of its institutions. Nonetheless, it remains true that no institutional change whatever can take place except if and when some people bring the change to pass.

                    *   *   *   *

As has just been pointed out, radical movements have endeavored to change popular attitudes in an effort to facilitate the coming of a socialist society of one kind or another. Their efforts have been largely unavailing, in many cases almost entirely futile. Anarchist and syndicalist propaganda has been severely limited in its results. The propaganda of the social democratic parties has at times been so ineffectual that some social democratic governments have not been able to rely on more than a limited degree of popular support. Indeed, many of those who have voted the social democratic tickets have done so out of sympathy, not with socialism, but with the liberal reformist programs espoused by the social democrats. Finally, the communists, exasperated by the failure of socialist propaganda, have resorted to terrorism and force.

What is responsible for the limited effectualness of radical propaganda? Part of the answer lies in this, that radicals have neglected to appeal to the best in human nature. They have not addressed themselves to the human spirit. They have assumed that little more was necessary than an appeal to economic needs and the love of power. They have been ignorant of this salient fact about human nature: human beings often respond more quickly to an appeal to their religion or their patriotism than to one addressed to their economic needs. Indeed, for the sake of religion or patriotism they will content themselves with minimal economic satisfactions. Radicals have not known this. Students of economics, political science and sociology, they have learnt a great deal about such things as production, distribution, profits, wages, rent, interest, dividends, law, courts, legislatures, strikes, pickets, injunctions—but of the human spirit they know next to nothing. Nor have they thought it necessary to know anything about it. According to their theory, human beings are swayed this way and that by things called social, economic and political forces, and it is therefore the latter, not the former, that it is important to know.

The matter does not end here. Something else enters into the picture. Radicals have not only failed to appeal to the best in human nature. They have taken care to appeal to the worst. They have appealed to the capacity for hate. They have preached the class struggle, and they have called upon men and women to hate, and to hate with all the passion at their command. Nothing else is needed to prove that radicals know nothing of the art of building a new world order. Nothing else is needed to establish the ethical immaturity of the radical. He does not seem to know that hatred and its inevitable concomitant, fear, corrode and corrupt and brutalize and disintegrate those who are dominated by them, and thereby unfit them for the task of building a superior society.

It is now possible to put a finger on one of the causes of the ethical failure of modern radicalism. Hate and fear are not creative forces; they destroy those who use them. They do not constitute the material out of which a new social order can be built. If it be argued that they are useful adjuncts in the dissolution of decadent social systems, it should be pointed out that when the haters put up a new system it tends to resemble the old in far too many particulars.

Modern radicalism has been prompted not by love of humanity, but by hatred of the old order and its rulers. This negative attitude makes considerable difference. Those who are motivated by little more than hostility toward the old system tend to respond to any and every revolutionary appeal, no matter by whom it is issued, without looking into the credentials of those who make the appeal, and often without any careful, critical examination of the revolutionary program. The results have been what might have been expected. Radicals are more gullible than they think. They follow fashions in revolution with about the same display of intelligence and independence as a woman shopper following fashions in dress. Thus, there was a time when radicals in certain countries flocked to the anarchist or syndicalist banner. In other countries, it was the flag of the social democracy.   Today communism is in style.   Some day it may be something else.

*   *   *   *

One of the greatest of radical blunders, and one of the chief reasons for the failure of radicalism, is the attempt to build a new world by the employment of means and methods that perpetuate the spirit of the old.

If I wish to rid myself of a bad habit, I must foster a better one. To do that I must alter my behavior; I must live the new pattern. But if instead I perpetuate the old behavior pattern, if I live that old pattern, the old habit will most certainly remain.

To attempt to build a new world by too excessive a reliance on precisely those behavior patterns, those attitudes, those scales of value which make the world the moral underworld it has always been, is to perpetuate that underworld and its spirit.   What are the results of a century of radical practice and preachment?   Not only is the world still a moral underworld, but what is most significant, radical movements, radical organizations and radical governments have themselves come to constitute a part of that underworld.   The history of every one of the great radical movements of the nineteenth and twentieth centuries is a story of political immorality.   They have exhibited exactly those political evils they ostensibly set out to abolish: the struggle for power, autocracy, hatred deliberately fostered, lying propaganda, the prostitution of culture, persecution, and too often violence, torture, and murder.

Whenever human beings strive for power and dominion, there the moral underworld will be found.   It has been truly said that power corrupts—to which may be added that the very quest for power corrupts.   There is nothing many people will not stoop to in their hunt for dominion.   Now if there is one old-world habit that radicalism has imitated with a vigor and a vim that are depressing to behold, it is the pursuit of power.   And in so doing radicalism ceased to be an instrument of moral progress.   One of the most essential ingredients of a morally superior society must be the diminution and, wherever possible, the elimination of government of human by human.   Such a society would indeed be democratic.   Nor would such a society be without government.   Government there would be, but it would be government with the accent on administration, rather than enjoyment of power.

To be fair to radicalism, there has been a radical movement that perceived all this: the anarchist movement.   To the anarchists should go the credit for possessing some of the best psychological insights of any radical movement—which may not be saying very much. The anarchists, better than any one else, have recognized politics for the immoral activity that it is. Better than other radicals they have perceived that the founders of a new world must first of all purify themselves of the power taint. Not that the anarchists have not sinned in this regard. But the insight is nevertheless valid. (This insight, it should be added, has been shared by many of those in the cooperative movement.)

Fairness to radicalism calls for still another concession. A group struggling to establish a better world will indeed find it necessary to acquire and employ political power at certain times and certain places. It may find such power a necessity for the gaining of ends that are desirable and that may not be gained otherwise. It may find such power necessary for the preservation of its right to exist and function as a group and of the right to spread its message and give expression to its ideals. In short, it may find a limited amount of political power useful and necessary. All this is granted. But most radicals have insisted on going far beyond this. They have pursued power and dominion with ruthless passion; they have demanded unlimited amounts of it; they have allowed themselves to be intoxicated by it whenever they have acquired it. In short, radicals have, in this matter, lived and assimilated and enjoyed too much of the old world to be effective agents and builders of the new. They suffer too much from the moral disease to be good moral physicians.

True it is that socialists and communists hold that the ultimate outcome of the socialist revolution will be a withering away of the organs of power and the emergence of the kind of society envisaged by the anarchists—a society composed of voluntary associations dedicated to the fulfillment of human wants. But here again radicalism reveals its ignorance of human nature. It is naive to suppose that any oligarchy, radical or otherwise, will willingly terminate its power —unless it is an oligarchy that knows that its doom is at hand.

❊　　❊　　❊　　❊

It is not at all surprising that modern radicalism, being lacking in spiritual insight, has always failed to understand religion and to grasp its profound significance for the human spirit. Not knowing religion, it fears it; fearing religion, it hates it; hating religion, it lays siege to it and seeks to exterminate it.

The radical conception of religion is crude and uncomprehending.

Being addicted to the class struggle conception of history, radicalism envisages religion as a political instrument. It is its function, on the one hand, to sanction the social order, to sanctify exploitation, and to render the masses more submissive; and, on the other, to guarantee to the exploited a happy and eternal life in the hereafter as a compensation for the brief and miserable existence here below. Religion becomes a sort of hypnotic, a device employed by the ruling classes to prepare the masses for exploitation, a weapon for the suppression of revolution, a consolation and compensation for the slave's miserable lot.

Modern radicalism being external, mechanical and institutionalist in outlook and approach, it misconceives religion accordingly. It envisages religion as an institution, a set of customs, a system of rites, rituals and beliefs, a priesthood, and a weapon in the struggle of the classes. But of the inner life of religion, of religion as spirit, of religion as a quest for ultimate meanings, modern radicalism knows nothing.

Its attack on religion constitutes one of radicalism's greatest and most tragic blunders. It has turned millions of men and women the world over into enemies of radicalism and radical change. No one will ever be able to compute the number of potential enemies of capitalism who were thereby turned into its steadfast defenders. It is needless to add that ruling classes everywhere have gleefully exploited the situation to the full. The blunder was as stupid as it was unnecessary.

One feels tempted to contemplate how different might have been the history of the nineteenth and twentieth centuries if the radical program had been offered to the world as part of a new religion, with a philosophy theistic, rather than atheistic and materialistic in character. The appeal of religion can be to the best in human nature. Further, its appeal is well-nigh universal. It addresses itself, not to any one group or class, but to all men and women. The new religion might have found acceptance, not only among the disaffected masses, but among many of the middle and upper classes as well. That social incubus known as the competitive economy might by this time have been a thing of the past. The world might have been spared a vast amount of suffering. But this is all speculation.

There is, however, no doubt that modern radicalism has been handicapped by its tie-up with materialism and atheism. It is of course an absurd superstition that atheists and materialists are necessarily lacking in spirituality. It is quite possible for an atheist or a materialist to create and appreciate spiritual values, and many of them do. But the tie-up of radicalism with atheism and materialism is most unfortunate, and not at all necessitated by any considerations of logic. Opposition to a competitive economy does not require an atheist or materialist metaphysics as a ground. Such opposition is not excluded by theism; there have been theists who have opposed private ownership in the means of production and distribution. A cooperative economy can be justified in terms of human needs; this is all the ground that is required. Such an economy can be defended on biological and psychological grounds. Logically neither theism, atheism or materialism are required. They are logically irrelevant. An opponent of a competitive economy or an advocate of a cooperative economy can therefore wear the atheist, or theist, or materialist, or any one of a number of other metaphysical labels.

❖   ❖   ❖   ❖

A survey of modern radicalism is a depressing experience. There seems to be no old-world vice that radicals have failed to perpetuate. Everything that radicals have been fond of classifying as symptomatic of moral decadence has been taken over by them, and with gusto and vim. Oppression and dictatorship, suppression of freedom, militarism and imperialism, terrorism and violence, prostitution of culture, lying propaganda, espionage and international intrigue—all these signify the complete moral bankruptcy of modern radicalism. It has succumbed to the very world it sought to save and is itself badly in need of salvation. It is part of the world's disease, and it is therefore absurd to think of it as the cure.

What a commentary on the ethical immaturity of millions of men and women that they actually look to modern radicalism to liberate them and to rid the world of its evils! In their blindness they do not perceive that modern radicalism and modern reaction are spiritually one. Both are foes of the human spirit. Both fear it and both conspire to smother it. Neither radicalism nor reaction has any use for goodness and truth and reason and sympathy and love.

To what conclusion is one led? It appears that one cannot look to modern radicalism for salvation. It is ethically too immature, spiritually too bankrupt to be entrusted with the task of building a new moral order. It may succeed, as it has in Russia, in tearing down old institutions and constructing new ones. But setting up a new social system is not the same as building a new moral order. The latter requires not only new institutions, but a new scale of values and a new spirit as well.

                    *   *   *   *

A new scale of values and a new spirit could be fostered by a society of men and women ethically, intellectually and aesthetically more mature than those that make up the vast majority of the world's population today. It is, however, a question whether a competitive economy conduces to such maturation. It may very well be that only a cooperative economy is capable of doing that.

10

CONFLICT THROUGH COMPETITION

If men and women are ever to approximate ethical, aesthetic and intellectual maturity, the world's way of life will have to be lifted from a preponderantly competitive to a prepotently cooperative level.

There are no two ways about it. There can be little ethical maturation in a preponderantly competitive society. In every such society that history has any record of, the mass of physically adult men and women has exhibited the traits of ethical immaturity. That this is so can be inferred from a reading of history and from the testimony of prophets, saints, philosophers and social reformers concerning the morality of their time and place. Always and everywhere their complaint is the same: immorality, selfishness, exploitation, slavery, violence, the hand of every one against every one. And everywhere and always, they find people enthralled by lies and deceptions, myths and delusions; being feared by every one, truth is unpopular.

What does this mean? It means that, judged by ethical and intellectual standards, competition is a failure. The competitive life is hostile to the good life, the full life, the life of the human spirit. It makes for the cramping and stunting of that spirit. This is unavoidably so. In a competitive society, every one is constantly preoccupied with the problem of survival—sheer physical survival. This results in a tremendous overvaluation of biological, economic, political and military values. In a competitive society, these are the dominant values, with ethical, aesthetic and intellectual values relegated to a secondary position, when they are not snuffed out altogether.

With very few exceptions, men and women will do anything to assure the physical survival of themselves and their loved ones. If necessary for survival, they will violate every tenet of the ethical code of their time and place, they will lie and deceive, they will tolerate the ugly.

Preoccupied with the problem of survival, the generality of men and women has little patience with, and less inclination for, the pursuit of ethical, aesthetic and intellectual values. Besides, the dominant values being biological, material and political, it is the acquisition of these that comes to be regarded by most people as the true measure of success, even of sanity. Indeed, the violation of the eth-

ical code and the manufacture of lies and deceptions, when performed
for the acquisition of material wealth and political power, come to be
regarded as evidences of a realistic and practical attitude. The evaluation of ethical, intellectual and aesthetic values as primary and the
attempt to guide one's life by means of such an evaluation, open one to
the suspicion of being impractical and unrealistic; they may even be
sufficient to brand one in the eyes of his fellows as insane.

It is unnecessary to add that in a competitive society the aesthetic
and the intellectual are often prostituted—they are bent to the ser-
vice of the material and the political.

Can a competitive society be anything else than a society of ethically stunted individuals? It is hard to see how it can. Competition,
by its very nature, breeds an excess of egotism and egotists. Those
who compete, compete to win—to win against others. Such an attitude cannot easily be dissociated from excessive egotism. Those
who lose in the struggle are often overcome by a sense of frustration.
The latter, too, makes for an accentuated egotism. To be humbled
is not the same as to acquire humility. One who is humbled too
often is likely to become anything but humble.

Those who assert that competition makes for individualism are con-
founding the latter with egotism. In actual fact competition does
not and cannot produce individuals, if by individuals is meant persons who are ethically, intellectually and aesthetically mature. The
plain fact of the matter is that no competitive society has ever made
the generation of such individuals its aim. The goal of every competitive society that ever was has been the enjoyment of material
wealth and political power. Such a society does not hesitate to
sacrifice individuals and individuality to attain its purpose. In such
a society, the great mass of individuals is just so much material for
powerful oligarchies to manipulate and exploit.

*   *   *   *

The indictment of competition is not yet complete. It cannot be
made complete without reference to a very important feature of
competition—its pathogenic character. A competitive society is a
sick society. It is physically and mentally sick. There is no need
here for mountains of statistics. Every one is acquainted with the
facts. Every one knows of the widespread incidence, even in normal
peacetime, of physical and neurotic illness. It is hard to avoid the
conclusion that the competitive way of life is largely responsible for
a great deal of our illness. The stresses and strains, the worries and

anxieties, the haste and hurry and frenzy, the sense of insecurity, the hatreds, panics and fears, all of which go with economic and political and military strife; the sense of frustration and the loss of self-confidence that go with defeat; and the inner conflicts that overtake those who face the temptation to violate the ethical code or who have yielded to the temptation: all these are pathogenic in character. This means they cannot be persisted in for too long a time without the setting in of a disease process. It is unnecessary to mention additional factors such as undernourishment and slum housing. Were everyone adequately fed, housed and clothed, physical, neurotic and mental illness would, of course, still be widespread for the reason that competition is in and of itself a pathogenic affair. Given competition on the economic, political and military levels, there will be stress and strain, worry and anxiety, hatred and fear, the sense of insecurity and the dread of failure, the sense of frustration and the loss of self-confidence, all topped by internal conflict. Given these, there will be illness, physical, neurotic and mental.

There will be those who will oppose the thesis that competition makes for an arrested personality. They will aver that it has an exactly opposite effect. Competition, they will insist, makes for growth. Rivalry stimulates effort, encourages self-improvement. It takes fitness to win and competition impels people to make themselves fit to win. Without competition there is stagnation.

Perhaps. But for what are the competitors competing? What is their goal? What are the prizes they seek? What values are they pursuing? Are their values biological, economic, political or military? Or are they ethical, aesthetic and intellectual?

Abstract discussions of fitness are useless. Those who win in a given struggle may be the fittest, but it may well be the case that the qualities that enable them to emerge victorious will not be the qualities that make for the enhancement of spiritual values. And this is indeed too often the case with competition on the economic, political and military levels. It is very often the case with the kind of competition in which physical survival itself is at stake. The fitness that emerges in the struggle for biological, economic, political and military values is not necessarily of the sort that makes its possessor an effectual instrument for the creation and appreciation of civilized values.

The fact of the matter appears to be, as has already been pointed out, that competitive societies are societies of spiritually immature men and women. This is the rock on which all arguments for competition break. Whatever else competition may fit a person for, it does not fit him for spiritual living. Indeed, competition is actually out of place where the spiritual is concerned. He who seeks ethical, aesthetic or intellectual values does not as a general thing envisage himself as a player in some kind of game in which the aim is to beat somebody. True enough, he may feel himself engaged in the severest sort of struggle with forces that are anti-spiritual in character. But this is a kind of competition that is unavoidable. Nor is it without its dangers. Always the spiritual warrior is beset by temptation. Strong is the temptation to win a cheap victory by a descent to the level of the anti-spiritual.

In actual fact, the spirit of competition is in a sense foreign to the realms of ethics, aesthetics and intellect. The worker in these fields is in quest of values of an intrinsic character. He is not working to roll up a score, but to create or possess something at least partly for its own sake. Goodness and truth and beauty are not prizes to be won in a competition; they are not in the same class with loving cups, bronze plaques, gold medals and blue ribbons. They are won by those who pursue them partly or wholly for their own sake and who regard their possession as sufficiently rewarding.

The worker in the realm of spirit may find it necessary to compete against forces of an anti-spiritual character, but this kind of competition can subsist on a level far different from that of the biological, economic, political or military sort. The spiritual warrior does not seek to exploit anyone, to amass wealth, or to set up dominion over others. He does not attempt to grow by denying growth to others. He does not try to liberate himself by enslaving another. In short, he does not practice spiritual cannibalism. He is in competition with competition itself. He is seeking to eliminate as much competition as possible in order to institute cooperation.

*   *   *   *

For thousands of years prophets and priests have been exhorting mankind to live up to the ethical standards set up by religion. Too often they seem to have thought that being ethical was just a matter of a simple exertion of the will. People could be good if only they made up their minds to. Everyone could ascend to a high moral level if he would make the effort.

Everyone knows how effectual the exhortations of priest and prophet have been. The generality of mankind has let them go unheeded. For this there is more than one reason, but only one need be mentioned here. It is this: a competitive way of life, as has already been pointed out, constantly poses a threat to one's physical existence. When the ordinary person's physical survival is at stake, he cannot be expected to exhibit any moral scruples to any great degree. He will do anything to survive, and if unethical practices help him to survive, then unethical he will be. He cannot be expected to sacrifice his welfare and his existence for the sake of a principle. The ordinary person is not, and cannot be expected to be, an idealist, a saint, a prophet or a martyr. He is to a limited degree a practical person, and he will do almost anything to survive and to satisfy his wants and those of his or her family. And when he observes that almost everyone around him is engaged in unethical practices, with himself and his family potential, if not actual victims, then the necessity for imitating his fellows becomes forcefully impressed upon him.

To all this must be added the further fact that the competitive way of life cannot but leave its impress upon character. Competition in the economic, political and military spheres tends to make men and women callous, indifferent to suffering, cruel. The callousness and cruelty affect, not so much one's relations with those that are near, as one's relations with humanity taken as a whole. This helps to explain why economic disaster, exploitation, starvation, squalor, war, disease, and other social evils become accepted parts of the social scene. One hears too many men and women refer to them as "part of the game." This is as good a way of evading one's moral responsibility as any.

What the competitive way does is to make unethical behavior habitual. It becomes ingrained in the personality . It becomes the mark of the "practical" man and woman, the "realistic" man and woman. The ethical life, the civilized way, come to be considered proper only for the "impractical" few, the "starry-eyed" idealists.

❊   ❊   ❊   ❊

The lesson is plain. The prophet must learn to heed the teachings of the psychologist and the sociologist. He cannot depend upon mere exhortation. If he does so, the chances are he will continue to go unheeded. Exhort he must and exhort he should, but he cannot stop there. He must help make the world a place in which it will be possible for the masses of men and women to practice the ethical life without jeopardy to their chances of physical survival. This means he must call on men and women to convert a preponderantly competitive order into one that is prepotently cooperative.

From the sociologist, the prophet and the religious leader must learn that when they deal with people, they have to deal with people who stand in certain relations to each other. Except by becoming hermits, people cannot step out of these relations. They mold these relations, but they are at the same time molded by them. It is these relations that constitute social institutions and social systems. Now, unless the prophet and the religious leader are prepared to advocate a change in the social system, it is useless for them to exhort people to adopt a kind of behavior that is at variance with the system they live under. It is useless for them to exhort people living under a preponderantly competitive system fully to practice a cooperative ethic. If it is the latter that the prophets and the religious leaders wish to see adopted, then they will have to have the courage of their convictions and become advocates of social change.

It seems certain that if the generality of men and women is to acquire spiritual maturity, our prepotently competitive way of life will have to yield to one that is preponderantly cooperative.

*   *   *   *

What kind of a cooperative society shall we seek? One in which the instruments of production are government-owned? No, for that would mean a society in which the psychological and spiritual maturation of the individual would find itself gravely threatened. It would mean a society in which material and political power would still enjoy a priority over ethical, intellectual and aesthetic values. A society in which industry is government-owned is a society governed by a wealth and power-hungry oligarchy. Enjoying the position of ruler, such an oligarchy will inevitably arrogate to itself as much wealth and as much power as it can.

A society of this sort might be cooperative, but it might also be a slave society. Cooperation in and of itself is not enough. It must be the cooperation of free men and women. It must be the cooperation of psychologically and ethically and intellectually mature human beings.

Unfortunately, the question of the competitive versus the cooperative society, like so many other questions, is being discussed on that intellectually impoverished level on which it is assumed that the choice is limited to two extreme alternatives. In this instance the choice is supposed to be between private ownership and government ownership. Since those who subsist on this impoverished level do not seem to be able to count more than two, it does not occur to them that there might be a third alternative. But a third alternative there is. This takes the form of ownership either by consumers, or by the workers, or both. An establishment might be owned by the consumers, as in the case of consumers' cooperatives, or it might be owned by those who work in it, or by both the workers and consumers.

Consumers' cooperatives have been in successful operation for over a century, so there can be no question concerning their practicability. They have proved themselves a success in every part of the world. As for entrusting the ownership and operation of an establishment to those who labor in it, it can be said in favor of the proposal that no one knows as much about the running of one as they who work in it. No one knows as much about railroading as railroad men. No one knows more about garment making than tailors.

This principle can be extended to other than industrial fields. Instead of either private or state medicine, cooperative medicine, with physicians, dentists, pharmacists, nurses, and consumers participating in ownership, might be instituted. Parents and teachers might learn to own and operate schools, adult students and teachers could run a college or adult education project. Actors, musicians, dancers and patrons could establish cooperatively-owned theatres, opera houses and orchestras. Authors are beginning to organize cooperative publishing houses.

One of the advantages of consumers' cooperation is this, that in many, if not most parts of the globe, it is possible to organize cooperatives without the fearful waste of time, energy and human life that attends the attempt to seek remedies through governmental action. In order to establish a cooperative it is usually not necessary to organize or bore into or capture a political party, or to beg favors of any politicians, or to win elections, or to capture a government, or to build barricades, or to overthrow, by force and violence, the rule of any oligarchy, or to establish a dictatorship. None of these things, so characteristic of behavior on the ethically immature level, are required. What are needed are the will, the social sagacity, and the enthusiasm.

Unfortunately, the organization of a society of worker-owned establishments presents difficulties with which consumers' cooperatives are not confronted. How shall private and corporate ownership be replaced by worker-ownership? The syndicalist proposal of a general strike aimed at compelling capitalists to relinquish their hold must be rejected as unrealistic and immature. Such a strike could very well lead to civil war and a revolutionary or counter-revolutionary dictatorship. Wars and dictatorships make people less, not more mature. They are the expression of life as it is lived on the level of ethical immaturity and collective paranoia. Further, it is idle to talk of dictatorships as temporary, transitional devices. Dictatorships tend to exhibit a most disconcerting passion for longevity. The syndicalists, like the socialists and the communists, propose eventually to abolish the state. The syndicalist strike proposal is, however, calculated to fixate the state, to prolong its existence, and to strengthen it immeasurably.

It is not possible to predict the future. The complex interplay of forces on the social level leads to the emergence of novel factors, factors possessed of characteristics that are unpredictable. The course of history has again and again been changed by just such forces. It is, however, permissible, while refraining from actual prediction, to describe possibilities. What may happen in the future is this: the current world trend toward government ownership and operation of economic facilities will be augmented. Statism, bureaucracy, loss of freedom will afflict nations and communities in many parts of the world. They will be endured for a while on the theory that they are necessary and transitory devices. They will tend to prolong their existence as long as possible. As they become increasingly intolerable, revolts, not necessarily violent, will flare up. But the world will not go back to private ownership. Labor and farmer unions and professional associations will step in and take over the ownership and operation of those economic facilities not already owned by consumer cooperatives.

A significant current development must be noted. In some European countries factory employee councils are in operation. The important thing about them is that the councils participate in the shaping of major policies. Through them the workers become partners in management and through them they learn to manage.

11

THE ETHICS OF COOPERATION

The fundamental class struggle—the struggle between the civilized minority and the uncivilized majority—stems in part from the fact that a society often has two sets of ideals: the professed ideals and the actually operative ones. The professed ideals—i.e., the ideals professed by society—are those that are actively pursued by the civilized minority. The conduct of the majority is governed by the ideals which place economic, political and military values in the forefront. The pursuit of civilized values is rejected as unrealistic and impractical, though the intellectual and aesthetic are sometimes sought as worthwhile secondary values, as hobbies, or as fashionable cultural possessions.

As has been pointed out, political radicals, though they esteem themselves civilizers, are in actual fact part and parcel of the majority —with some exceptions, of course. Radicals hunger chiefly for power. They profess great admiration for ethical, intellectual and aesthetic values, but the pursuit of these values is to be postponed until the "better" society is established. The spiritual revolution must wait. The spiritual revolution is off indefinitely.

What a pity it is that the radical movements of modern times— socialism, communism, syndicalism, and anarchism—though in re- socialism. communism. syndicalism and anarchism—though in re- bellion against almost everything else, have persistently refused to break with what has constituted the worst aspect of life in past and present societies. Heretics with reference to almost everything else, they have chosen to remain orthodox with reference to the one thing that more than anything else has cried out for rebellion.

Throughout the history of all except a number of primitive so- cieties, a certain behavior-pattern has been dominant. Almost every individual has been educated to respond to other individuals in terms of conflict, rather than cooperation. He or she has been brought up to prefer the way of conflict, competition, war, exploitation, hate, as against the way of cooperation, democracy, love, charity, sympathy, generosity and magnanimity. He has been taught that whenever it is a choice between the two, the former, the way of conflict, is to be chosen. He has been told that this is a sign of strength. Individuals, groups, governments, institutions of all kinds, even the churches, were to favor the harsh way.

History has therefore been to a large extent a story of conflict and competition, of fighting and war, of cruelty and hate. It has been in great part a sustained cry of agony, of suffering and pain.

To explain how this has come about many have resorted to either one of two kinds of mystagogy: the internal and the external kind. Those who have recourse to internal mystagogy posit a mysterious entity residing in the innermost depths of the human spirit. This entity is variously called radical evil, original sin, human perverseness, essential corruption, aggressive instinct. This demonic entity is supposed to impel human beings to acts of self-aggrandisement, to destruction, to all sorts of diabolical deeds.

No one has ever succeeded in demonstrating the existence of this inner spook.

Others prefer the mystagogy of the external kind. They speak of social forces or institutions, conceived as existing in some upper atmosphere and apart from human beings, human wills and human motives, and compelling men and women, against their will, to do all sorts of wicked things. Thus, military institutions are supposed to compel peace-loving peoples to make war against each other. A competitive economic order compels unselfish, generous and high-souled people to exploit each other. There are social forces and institutions, but the existence of the kind now under discussion has never been demonstrated. There are no social forces or institutions apart from human beings acting in concert or opposition. Social forces and institutions are expressions of the spirit actuating the people of a community. They are human beings standing in certain relations to each other.

Rejecting all mystagogy, let it be noted that human society has been preponderantly competitive, exploitative and authoritarian. Let due note also be taken of the unbelievable material and moral squalor in which most human beings have lived throughout recorded history. It then becomes legitimate to suppose that the majority of men and women have been immature—immature ethically, volitionally, emotionally, intellectually. They have been immature, unintegrated, when not disintegrated. What other result could there be? Given a society that is preponderantly competitive, exploitative and authoritarian; in which everyone is at war with everyone; in which everyone strives to grow at the expense of the growth of everyone else; in which biological, economic and political values are deemed primary, and ethical, religious, aesthetic and intellectual values are pushed into the background; in which the masses of men and women spend lives steeped in material and moral squalor; given such a society and it is highly probable that the majority of its men and women will be psychologically and spiritually immature.

This description probably fits every Occidental and Oriental society throughout recorded history.

If history has been what it has, it has been what might have been expected of a world of men and women of arrested personalities.

For thousands of years prophets and priests, rabbis and ministers, saints and martyrs, ethical and social reformers have preached and exhorted and implored men and women to live up to the professed ideals of their religions and societies. As a rule their appeals have been ineffectual. Addressed as they were to the psychologically and ethically immature, to those whose behavior-patterns had been fashioned by life in competitive, exploitative and authoritarian societies, no other result could have been expected. Further, as was pointed out in the preceding chapter, there is little use in asking men and women to exhibit ethical behavior when the economic security and survival of themselves and their loved ones are threatened, as they constantly are in a competitive society. It cannot be too strongly emphasized that most men and women will do anything to ensure the survival and economic security of themselves and their loved ones. When unethical behavior is felt to be necessary to achieve this end, unethical behavior is resorted to.

In the light of all this, history has been just what it might have been expected to be. It is therefore unnecessary to have recourse to radical evil, mystagogic social forces or cyclical theories of the rise and fall of civilizations, to explain the course history has taken. These fictions are called upon because thought about human affairs is dominated by the stereotyped notion that the physically mature have throughout history been psychologically, that is, emotionally, intellectually and volitionally mature as well. It is assumed that everybody grows into psychological maturity "naturally," independently of the environing social order.

If one proceeds on this stereotyped assumption, if one takes it for granted that the physically adult have also been psychologically mature, then history becomes altogether inexplicable. The question, why have men and women done so much evil, becomes unanswerable. Faced with this mystery, philosophers, historians, ethicists, social scientists and almost everyone else have relied on stereotyped mystagogic explanations, such as those just mentioned. It is sometimes sought to explain evil in terms of ignorance, or the dominance of passion and emotion. But it is always the ignorance or the passions and emotions of supposedly psychologically mature men and women that is meant.

The anthropologists, sociologists and psychologists who insist that the individual's behavior-pattern is shaped by the culture of his or her time and place are probably close to the truth. But their finding needs to be supplemented by the perception that a culture not only shapes an individual's behavior-pattern; it may also operate to facilitate or obstruct his psychological maturation. No reason exists for the assumption that an individual matures "naturally," and that he does so be the environing culture what it may.

✻   ✻   ✻   ✻

It has just been asserted that the dominant behavior-pattern in all except a few primitive societies has been one that stressed conflict, competition and exploitation. Individual and group interests are, it has been thought, best secured by a constant state of war against other individuals and groups.

Modern radicalism, as has been seen, in its attempt to replace a competitive by a cooperative social order, has made the fatal error of supposing that authoritarianism, intolerance, class hatred, conflict and war could tend to facilitate the creation of a society of men and women whose dominant behavior-pattern would be one of cooperation, democracy, freedom, sympathy and love. Radicalism rebels against the competitive society, but not against the competitive spirit. Its rebellion is therefore a superficial affair. It destroys the institutions built by the competitive spirit, but, because it is itself an expression of that spirit, it replaces them with institutions and ways of life that perpetuate the old world. Modern radicalism is therefore basically conservative. It cannot bring the new world into being. It is not a remedy; it is itself a part of the disease.

Centuries upon centuries, millennia upon millennia of wrong living have brought the world to its present pass. Today's crisis, all myths to the contrary notwithstanding, is not due to any departure from the spirituality and morality of the past. There was very little spirituality and morality in the past to depart from. This fact is concealed from view by the almost universally accepted stereotyped notion that the men and women of past eras subsisted on a truly spiritual and ethical plane. There is not the slightest warrant for such a belief. The history of the recorded past is in very large part the story of spiritual squalor and of exploitation, selfishness and the war of all against all. Competition, exploitation, war, authoritarianism, hate, fear, intolerance, cruelty: these have been in large part the way of the world.

They have failed, all of them. Civilization there has been—in spite of them, not because of them. Civilization has in large part been created and sustained by that minority of men and women who have actively pursued religious, ethical, aesthetic and intellectual values, men and women who to a greater or lesser degree deviated from prevalent behavior-patterns that called for the active pursuit of wealth and power. The existence of civilization through so many millennia is a demonstration of the superiority of their way of life.

It has always been the destiny of this minority to play a prophetic role and by precept and example to teach humanity how to live. Humanity has, alas, not yet learned who its best teachers are; it has not yet learned to heed its prophets. But the way of conflict has failed. It must fail, for it can breed only a humanity composed, in the main, of arrested personalities. Only the way of cooperation, democracy, love, reason, and art can foster a humanity composed of mature personalities.

Those who follow this way are the true radicals, as they are also the true conservatives. To follow this way, to become a true radical, a genuine conservative, it is necessary to liberate oneself from the thralldom of intense group loyalties and the slavery of doctrine, creed and party line. The ethical and intellectual transcendentalism that unites one with all men and women everywhere, frees the self. Thus it comes about that in acquiring a universal outlook, one becomes more completely individual. But it is necessary to do more. It is necessary to cultivate cooperative, democratic, magnanimous ways and to do so until they become fixated in an enduring behavior-pattern. For the majority of men and women this change may need to be facilitated by a corresponding transformation of the environing social system. It is necessary for the civilizers to facilitate such a transformation in every way that is consistent with their ideals.

*   *   *   *

One of the characteristics of the civilized minority is its ability to distinguish between spirit and the instruments and symbols of spirit. A large part of the world's confusion and tragedy is traceable to the inability of most men and women to make a distinction between things of the spirit and "things" of the spirit.

12

"THINGS" OF THE SPIRIT

There are things of the spirit and there are *the things* of the spirit. The sad fact is that most people are best acquainted with the latter, *the things*. The sadder fact is that most people confound the two. There is no calculating the terrible harm wrought to the life of the spirit and the life of humanity by the almost ubiquitous failure to distinguish between the two.

Spirit has its instruments and symbols, its rites and rituals. These are its "things." Spirit should, however, never be confounded with the latter. But confounded they have been, and by almost everybody everywhere. Practically universal has been the tendency to think that spiritual living means the performance of certain rites and rituals, or a preoccupation with certain instruments and symbols.

The situation is not without its element of irony. The confusion often extends to the point where they who do distinguish between spirit and its "things," and who keep the former while discarding the latter, are denounced as unspiritual or anti-spiritual and subjected to persecution!

There is no department of the life of spirit where this tragic confusion does not reign. To commence with that which the prophets of all times and places have condemned with all the vigor and vehemence at their command: the failure to distinguish between religion, which is spirit, and its "things." Being religious has too often been defined, in practice, as church attendance, ritual performance, mechanical utterance of prayer, participation in church activities, keeping of feasts, fasts and holidays, and the prominent display of cross, star, crescent or some other symbol. These have been called being religious, being spiritual. The fact of the matter is, of course, they are not the distinctive signs of either.

The teaching of religion to children is also termed being religious. But such teaching involves their indoctrination with theological notions and the acquisition of the routine habits just described. The result of such an education may very well be and too often is the generation of "religious" automata. Such pedagogy hardly deserves the appellation of religious or spiritual.

There is a great deal of commotion today over the question of starting the school day with a prayer or a reading of the Bible, as well as the question of released time for the indoctrination of school children in theological beliefs. This is called introducing religion in the public schools. It is nothing of the sort. It should be spoken of as the introduction into the public schools of the mechanics of religion.

If one turns to patriotism, one notes a confusion that is exactly analogous to that which prevails in religion. Patriotism, which is spirit, is confounded with its instruments and symbols, its rites and rituals. As a consequence, many a person who violates his or her country's laws without so much as a scruple, esteems himself or herself patriotic if he or she waves or displays the flag, stands when the national anthem is played, takes off his hat when the flag passes by, keeps the national holidays (by a trip to a resort), indulges in braggadocio about his or her nation, and contemns those who had the misfortune to be born in another country. None of these are the distinctive marks of patriotism as spirit.

The confusion under consideration has, in this so-called scientific age, kept people from understanding the meaning and import of science. Science, which is spirit, is identified with its instruments and certain of its procedures. Many a teacher of science, many a worker in a scientific laboratory, think themselves scientific because they employ scientific instruments, perform experiments, use scientific terms and sling scientific equations. They esteem themselves scientific even though they may manifest intolerance and bigotry, and even though their interest in science as spirit be so slight that they will not take the trouble to acquaint themselves with the philosophy of science. How many scientists can discuss competently and intelligently, the metaphysical presuppositions of their science, the concept of scientific law, the concept of cause, the criteria of truth, the logic of science, and so on?

That this confusion is dangerous is proved by the hostile attitude exhibited by very many people to the employment of the scientific approach to psychological and social problems. An analysis of their arguments reveals a failure to distinguish between the scientific temper and the tools that science employs. Thus, it will be argued that one cannot put human beings in test tubes, that psychological and social phenomena are not always subject to precise measurement, that measurement and statistics are anyway not the key to the understanding of human nature and society. But test tubes, measurements and statistics are not science; they are merely its tools. When scientists propose that science be brought to bear on psychological and social problems, they are thinking in terms of science as spirit: the spirit that is manifested in the search for truth arrived at by the employment of objective criteria, systematic observation and experiment, rational as against emotionally charged hypotheses and theories, mistakenly regarded as absolute truths or eternal verities—the spirit that transcends party lines, "isms," doctrines, creeds, slogans and stereotypes.

Science is a department of culture, using this term in the narrow sense as comprising art, literature, religion, science and philosophy. Culture is spirit and is to be distinguished from its instruments: books, lectures, schools, concerts, theatres, clubs, forums, etc. This distinction is rarely observed. As a result, a preoccupation with any or all of these things is mistakenly regarded as a sign of culture. The confusion is most unfortunate. Such a preoccupation is not necessarily a sign of culture. Everything depends on the spirit in which these instruments of culture are employed.

It is not a sign of culture to read best sellers because they are best sellers, or to read a book for no other reason than that it is the latest, or one of the latest, while neglecting books that are months, years, decades, generations or centuries old. It is not necessarily a sign of culture to immerse oneself in a book to escape from reality. It is not necessarily a sign of culture to attend concerts, plays, or lectures simply because that is the thing to do in one's set.

What is the culture of a person who reads the latest books and all the best sellers, but has never held communion with a great book? What is the culture of a person who attends lectures, plays and concerts, but cannot discuss any of them intelligently?

In fine, preoccupation with the instruments of culture is not necessarily a sign of culture. Everything depends on the spirit with which the instruments in question are used. Culture is spirit—spirit manifesting itself in a passion for truth, for beauty, for art.

There is yet another realm in which the confusion between spirit and rite and ritual is evident. The ritual of respect is too often mistaken for the spirit of respect. Respect has its rites and rituals: the handshake, the doffing of the hat, the salute, the bow, the rising from one's seat, the wearing of garments suitable to the occasion, the you-go-first procedure, and so on. Some of the rites are sensible, others succeed in stultifying human relations. It is absurd to assume that the performance of the rite of respect is necessarily a sign that the spirit of respect is present. Yet the pathetic fact remains that those who perform the rites, in no matter how mechanical a manner, are often certain that they have given evidence of genuine respect.

Genuine respect is spontaneous. It cannot be willed. It is impossible to will to respect that which does not invite respect. Conventional respect is therefore likely to be little more than a kind of play-acting. One behaves as if one were giving expression to the spirit of respect. The one who is the recipient of this kind of respect may or may not be deceived. If the latter is the case, he or she may take the cue and respond in kind. The entire procedure will then be nothing more than a contribution to the art of histrionics.

✳   ✳   ✳   ✳

It is not proposed to abolish rituals, rites and symbols. A certain amount of symbolism, a certain amount of ritualism, are unavoidable, perhaps even desirable. Two things need to be done, however. Rituals, rites and symbols should be reduced to the barest minimum necessary. The experience of the Quakers, Unitarians and the Society for Ethical Culture suggests that a minimum is sufficient. Complicated, cumbersome, top-heavy, energy and time-consuming rites and rituals are not at all necessary. In addition, they are dangerous, encouraging as they do an excessive devotion to and preoccupation with the mechanical and external evidences of spirit.

The second reform necessary is the education of people in the distinction between spirit and the instruments and symbols of spirit. It is necessary for people to learn that the value of instruments and symbols is, in part at least, extrinsic and derivative. An instrument derives its value as instrument from the end which it subserves. A symbol derives its value from that which it symbolizes. The ritualistically-minded person is likely to regard the symbol as possessed of some mysterious intrinsic value. The person who risks life and limb to save a flag from being destroyed has not matured to the point of distinguishing between the flag and that for which it stands. For him the flag has a value that is intrinsic, rather than extrinsic. The person who is angered by the defilement of a symbol and who remains apathetic in the face of the defilement of the principles symbolized is both ethically and intellectually immature. For him too, value resides in the symbol rather than that which the symbol represents.

Symbols and rituals can be dangerous. They can loom so large as to crowd out spirit. They can and do become a substitute for spirit. They must be used with caution. Everyone who is to employ

them should be educated in their proper use. Further, everyone
should be taught that spirit is enough, that refusal to employ rite
and symbol is not necessarily a sign of indifference or opposition to
spirit—it may even be an indication of the presence of spirit. Education in the employment of ritual and symbol should be accompanied
by a cultivation of a tolerant attitude toward those who do without
them.

✿   ✿   ✿   ✿

It is sad to contemplate the fact that human beings the world over
seem always to have entertained an external, mechanical view of the
life of spirit. It is a melancholy fact that the latter has too often been
conceived as a going through certain motions, or a preoccupation
with certain material objects. In the last few years many American
communities have indulged in a great deal of fretting and fuming
caused by the refusal of children of parents belonging to a religious
sect known as Jehovah's Witnesses to salute the American flag. If
these children were to salute the flag, while exhibiting little or no
interest in the things the flag stands for, there would be a great deal
less fretting and fuming. In all parts of the world it has always been
safer to violate every principle of morality and religion than to do
violence to the symbols thereof. It is more dangerous to defile the
flag and the cross than the principles the flag and the cross represent.

It seems a strange thing that humanity should mistake preoccupation with the rituals and instruments of spirit for spiritual living itself.
It may seem incredible that any one could confuse the two, and yet
the confusion seems to have obtained everywhere and always. Had
it been otherwise, the history of humanity would have been a very
different sort of thing, and the prophets of all times and places would
have had much less to inveigh against.

Among the things that prophets have denounced is precisely this
substitution of instrument and rite for spirit. And whenever they
have done this, they have been classed as enemies of spirit, and as
themselves something less than spiritual! What prophet has not
been charged with being such? As if this were not enough, the
persecution, yes, the crucifixion of the prophet may come to be considered services to spirit!

History knows no irony greater than that exhibited by the fate of
the prophet.

The persecution of a prophet sometimes leads to unexpected results. The persecutors acquire a sense of guilt. By way of expiation,
the persecutors may convert the persecuted prophet and his ideals into

objects of worship. A whole new set of rites and rituals will then be instituted, to be performed in precisely the mechanical manner the prophet denounced. Irony is thus added to irony while saints shake their heads.

13

THE MEANING OF IT ALL

In the first chapter it was stated that there appears to be a hierarchy of being which seems to subsist on eight levels: inanimate matter, viruses, one-celled organisms, cell colonies, plants, conscious animals, human beings, and civilized human beings. It was also asserted that in a rough way this represents the course of evolution, with the civilized stage the highest level attained to date. What, now, is the meaning of this evolutionary process?

One may hold, as many do, that it is all an accident. From this standpoint, every stage is the resultant of a purely fortuitous coincidence of forces. Things just happen. Humanity simply owes its existence to a happy or unhappy series of coincidences, depending on one's point of view. The accidentalist position may be correct, but there appears to be no way of validating it.

Or one may, with the materialists, assert that it is all rooted in the inherent properties of matter: everything is material, the potentialities of all things are contained in primitive matter. This proposition is to be rejected as false. Consciousness is not material. Ideas are not material. Art, science, philosophy, literature, religion are not material. To which the materialist can reply that consciousness, ideas, art, science, philosophy, literature, and religion are never found separate from matter. Consciousness requires an organism, ideas a brain, art, science, philosophy, literature and religion material media. This may be true, but the materialist is a poor metaphysician. For some reason or other, he seems to be unable to distinguish between separation and distinction. Assuming it to be true that mind and its products are inseparable from matter, the fact remains that they are distinguishable from it. Consciousness is distinct from body, ideas from brain, a philosophy from the paper it is written on, the spirit of art, science, philosophy, literature and religion from the material instruments and symbols employed.

The materialist philosophy itself, like every other philosophy, like every other idea or system of ideas, is non-material in character.

It is not easy to see in primitive matter—in, say, electrons, protons, neutrons, or the pre-solar system nebula—the potentialities of consciousness and of symphonies, epic poetry, philosophical systems, scientific thought and deeds of love.

The trouble with the materialist is that his gaze is riveted upon the first, the material stage, of evolution. He is fascinated by matter and he cannot take his eyes off it.

Another interpretation of the course evolution has taken is that offered by the emergent evolutionists. They hold that each stage of the evolutionary process has laws of its own, and that the phenomena found on any stage are not completely interpretable by laws that are valid for those on other levels. This is another way of saying that the behavior of entities subsisting on a given evolutionary level is to be explained in terms of the structures and properties of the entities in question. This sounds sensible. Such a procedure avoids the fallacy of reductionism, the "nothing but" type of explanation. It recognizes that evolution involves more than a mere rearrangement of forces. A rearrangement of forces, or a novel combination of factors may issue in the emergence of an entity with a unique and unpredictable set of properties. One may be tempted, with the creative evolutionist, to see in all this the work of a creative force, nisus, will or elan vital, blind or intelligent. Emphasis will then be laid on the creative act. The emphasis is unfortunate. If one assumes such a will to be at work, its creative activity is not an end, but a means. It does not create for the sake of creation. Creation exists for the sake of the things created, not for itself.

Creative persons are often—too often—described as indulging in creation for its own sake, but this is an oversimplification. The creative person is greatly concerned about the product of his activity. This product is usually and hopefully regarded by its creator as a permanent contribution to the store of civilized values: to art, literature, science, philosophy, religion, or ethical or social reform, as the case may be. A creator brings into being value-carrying entities, not trifles or transient wares; at least, that is his ambition.

If there is a creative cosmic force at work, its products are apparently not trifles. If it is an intelligent force, its concern with the events that take place on all levels of reality must be great indeed.

The holists and their allies speak of a nisus toward the formation of wholes, integers, unities. They point to the fact that evolution often proceeds by the union of entities to form entities of a larger and more comprehensive sort: atoms unite to form molecules, cells make up an organism, organisms a society, societies a federation, and so on. This is true, but here again the emphasis is unfortunately placed. The important thing about an entity is not that it is one, not that it is a whole, but the kind of entity it is. There may be more unity in a triangle than in many a painting, but that is no reason for preferring the triangle. There may be more wholeness in many a mediocre person than there is in many a genius, but the latter is nonetheless a more important sort of person. There is a great deal of fuss being made nowadays over wholes, unities, integrity and oneness. These things are undoubtedly important, but it is doubtful if it is legitimate to speak of a cosmic nisus toward oneness as such. The trend may be there, but if one may conceive of a cosmic impulsion that envisages unity as its goal, it may not be unity for the sake of unity, but for the sake of the values that unity may subserve. Mere arithmetical oneness can hardly be considered as the grand aim for which the cosmic impulsion strives.

Is there some sort of a force or nisus at work, and is it intelligent? Religious people say there is, and they add that it is not only intelligent, but just and loving as well. In this respect, the religious person is at the opposite pole from the materialist. If the latter's gaze is riveted on matter, the lowest known level of reality, the religious person's gaze is directed toward higher values and those who create them—the highest known level of reality. It is in terms appropriate to this level that he conceives the ultimate principle, which he terms God. He thus runs the risk of being called anthropomorphic, but he replies quite sensibly that, if deity is to be conceived at all, it is to be conceived in terms appropriate to the highest known level of being. These may fall far, far short of accuracy and adequacy, but they are the best terms at his disposal and it is conceded that their descriptive value is anyway asymptotic.

Is there any way of demonstrating the truth of any of these interpretations? Apparently not. One wishes it were possible to establish the religious interpretation, but this seems out of the question. The mystic is certain that he has touched deity, but his claim is, alas, not subject to objective verification. It is legitimate to regard the existence of a personal deity as a possibility, perhaps a probability. Is it possible to go farther than this? One wishes it were, but it is difficult to see how. As nearly as can be made out, there exists no organon by the use of which the question of the existence of deity might be resolved. Intuition, reason, mystic communion, the doctrine of revelation: none of these satisfy. The believer falls back on what he terms faith, but the latter seems to be little more than a resolve to accept the existence of that the existence of which is undemonstrable. It may very well be that what is called faith should in some instances be labeled hope: one hopes that the cosmos is after all a divinely guided affair. And there is ground for hope. It is legitimate to suppose that a universe that is so incredibly, inconceivably great, a universe that is so varied and complex, a universe the parts of which fit so wonderfully well together, may be something more than a mere accident, or something that is, and is for no particular reason at all. It is legitimate to suppose that the progression from matter through virus and cell and cell colony and plant and animal and human to civilizer may be more than a surge of blind forces, more than a pitiless grinding and rolling, more than a carrier of local and transient values and meanings. It is permissible to hope that the cosmos is not a spiritual desert, a spiritual waste-land; that it is instead the work of a Being Who knows and understands and loves and Who endows the entire universe with a meaning and a value that are eternal.

14

THE PRIMACY OF BEING

Being strives to perpetuate itself and to be as full and complete as possible.

It appears to be true, generally, that all instances of being seek to perpetuate themselves—to exist as long as possible. Being strives to be, to continue being. This may not be true of the meson, a cosmic ray particle that is said to last only a fraction of a second, but if the meson's span of life is no longer than this, it does not follow that the striving is not there. Evidently the meson exists no more than a fraction of a second because this is as long as it is able to. Moreover, a fraction of a second may be a long time from the meson's standpoint. A span of time that seems much too brief to a human being may seem quite long to a being of another kind.

There is, of course, the fact of suicide. The person who commits suicide is terminating his being. So is the person who is sacrificing his life for another or for a cause. But these cannot be cited as disproof of the statement concerning the self-perpetuating urge of being. The suicide, the hero and the martyr would like to continue living; only circumstances, inner or outer, keep them from doing so. The desire to continue existing is present. However, this may not be true of the melancholiac suicide. But then, as has just been pointed out, every instance of being strives not only to be, but to be full and complete. The hero and the martyr feel that though their existence is being terminated, it is also being enriched and made meaningful by the heroism or the martyrdom. The person committing suicide does so precisely because he feels, rightly or wrongly, that his life has not been as full, as complete as he would like it to be.

It may therefore be affirmed that, as a general thing, every entity strives to exist as long as possible. Spinoza may have had this in mind when he said something to the effect that every entity seeks to institutionalize itself. Spinoza is right. Every instance of being, as a general thing, seeks to perpetuate itself, to become an institution, a fixture, an enduring object.

The cosmos is being. Everything in it strives to be, and to be as long as possible.

All of the foregoing will be found party or wholly unacceptable by the process philosophers. Ever since Heraclitus, and perhaps before him, there have been philosophers who place great stress on process. For them there is no being, there is only becoming. There are no entities, there are only events. All is process, all is change, all is motion and flow. Nothing endures. The universe is not a static affair; it is a dynamic, evolving phenomenon.

A philosophy that says all is process, all is change, nothing endures, cuts the ground from under itself. If nothing endures, then it follows that at every moment an entirely new universe comes into being, a universe that has no connection with the one preceding and the one following. But if this is the case, then there is no change, no process, no becoming; there is only a succession of states.

If nothing endures, then in the case of any entity it can be said that at every moment an entirely new entity comes into being, and one that has no connection with the one preceding and the one following. But again, if this is the case, there is no process, no evolution; there is only a succession of states.

The fact of the matter is that every process philosophy does assume the existence of an eternal, unchanging something. A philosophy that stresses change will assume the existence of laws of change that do not themselves change. The laws of evolution do not evolve, although concepts of them may. There can be no exclusive process philosophy without self-contradiction at its heart. Heraclitus, the philosopher of change, postulated the existence of a fundamental Reason that did not itself change, but governed all change. Spencer, the philosopher of evolution, assumed an invariant law of evolution, and Bergson, another evolutionary philosopher, assumed the existence of an enduring elan vital that guided evolution.

If a philosophy is to be coherent, it must postulate the existence of some kind of invariant fact. Every system of ideas must be built around some sort of an absolute.

What is perhaps the most useless revolt in the history of philosophy is the revolt against the absolute. What makes the revolt useless is the fact that no one can do without an absolute. The rebels themselves are living proof of this, for they too have their absolutes.

Every philosophy has its absolute. This is true of the philosophy of the professional philosopher and of that of the ordinary man and woman. It is probably impossible to think a philosophy minus an absolute. It is easy to see why. A philosophy, to be a philosophy, must be more or less coherent. There must be some coherence in it somewhere. A philosophy in which all thoughts contradict each other is hardly thinkable. But what gives a philosophy whatever coherence it does possess? What makes its parts hang together? The answer is, some principle, some fundamental thought, some basic idea. The principle permeates the philosophy; the latter is the expression of it. In the philosophy the principle functions as a constant, an invariant, an absolute. It knits the philosophy together, makes it into a system.

Every philosophy is a universe of discourse. Within that universe the principle functions as an absolute. This is true of all philosophies, including those that term themselves anti-absolutist. An anti-absolutist philosophy, if it is at all coherent, will be knit together by some principle, some basic tenet. Within the universe of discourse constituted by an anti-absolutist philosophy, the integrating principle will function as an invariant, an absolute.

The absolute of any philosophy always has, or purports to have, an external reference. The reference is to a fact, real or alleged, of cosmic importance. This fact, basic to the philosophy, is conceived to be basic to the universe as well. It knits the cosmos together, makes it in some sense a whole, as it makes the philosophy a whole. The fact in question may be God, the dialectic, matter, cosmic mind, the elan vital, a society of immortal spirits, a law of change, creative activity, a nisus toward unity and wholeness, and so on, and so on. Be the basic fact what it may, it will be envisaged as universal, eternal and invariant. Some may protest and say they depict their central fact as itself undergoing variation and growth. These will, however, be found to describe variation and growth as governed by laws that are themselves envisaged as unchangeable. These laws then constitute the invariant fact, the absolute.

A survey of philosophies that call themselves anti-absolutist would reveal them as possessed of absolutes. Naturalism accepts the laws of nature as invariant. Pragmatists hold that a proposition is true if its application to a situation leads to the expected consequences. The proposition is then held to be applicable to all essentially similar situations. This presupposes the essential repeatability of situations. A situation that has occurred once may occur again. Were this not the case, education would be useless. Education presupposes the repeatability of situations. If fire occurred only once in the history of the universe, there would be no point in teaching anyone how to control a fire. If the first case of pneumonia in the history of the cosmos were also the last, it would be a waste of time teaching physicians how to treat the disease. Pragmatism thus presupposes a certain amount of invariance in the universe, as does also every philosophy of education.

Relativism presupposes an absolute. Thus, in the case of physical relativism, when it is maintained that space, time and motion are relative to an observer at a point in a given frame of reference, invariance enters when it is urged that space, time and motion are the same for every observer at the given point. Similarly, in the case of cultural relativism, when it is argued that cultural values differ with place and time, invariance enters when it is pointed out that every person born into and reared in a given culture at a given time will to some degree imbibe its values.

There is no need to labor the point. Every philosophy is built around some basic concept. The latter makes the philosophy a more or less coherent whole. It makes it possible to say that there is something in the last sentence of the philosophy which is there in the first. The basic concept functions as an invariant, an absolute.

* * * *

Process philosophies envisage process as an ultimate, a basic fact. It is a question whether process is that. Process, change, evolution, development, motion and flow are rather the properties of things. There is no process, no change, no evolution apart from entities. There is no becoming apart from being. No one ever saw a case of pure, abstracted becoming or process or change.

The retort will be made that no one ever saw an instance of pure being, being without process, without change. Everything, it will be asserted, is in process of changing, be the alteration ever so imperceptible. However, speech and thought are in large part built around the idea of the priority of being. Thus, when a plant grows, the growth is said to be happening to the plant. One does not speak of the plant as something that happens to the growth. When a person falls ill, the illness is spoken of as happening to him. One does not speak of him as something happening to the illness. It seems more sensible to suppose that change occurs to an entity than to suppose that an entity occurs to change. However, one speaks of evolution as having stages. Here language seems to recognize process as ultimate. But what happens between stages? Evolution? Evolution of what? It has already been pointed out that, in the absence of an enduring entity, there is no evolution, only a succession of states, with no state connected in any way with the one preceding and the one following.

To this the reply may be made that process, evolution, growth and change are not discontinuous; they are continuous. There are no temporal gaps, no discrete moments, and there is therefore no succession of states. But I do not know whether it has been conclusively demonstrated that all things are always and everywhere continuously undergoing change.

There is no denying the reality of process. Becoming is real. There is, however, plenty of evidence that being too is real. The empirical evidence favors the view that something endures through change. There is something in the present which has survived from the past and is entering into the future. There is something in the last act of a play which was there in the preceding acts, and which gives the play its unity. There is something in the last thought of a system of philosophy which is there in the first and makes it possible to say the system is one. No matter how greatly a person or an organized group of persons may change, one can discern in him or it enduring complexes of aspects or traits. Habit, memory and tradition can persist for a very long time. The universe itself, in spite of all the change that goes on in it, remains essentially the same. We recognize it as essentially the same universe we knew an hour ago, yesterday, last week, last month, a year ago, a decade ago, a generation ago. According to astronomers' and geologists' accounts, the universe has in certain fundamental respects been always the same.

Indeed, one of the most remarkable things about this cosmos is the persistence so many things exhibit. Now one of the things that makes for persistence is the fact of organization. When entities unite to form a larger and more inclusive entity, they may reenforce and strengthen each other. They then conserve each other's being, as well as that of the larger entity itself. The bond of union may be strong enough to make the dissolution of the larger entity an extremely difficult affair. A good instance of this is the atom. Every one knows how difficult it is to break up an old habit or to rid oneself of a prejudice of long standing. It is not the age of the habit or the prejudice that is responsible for the difficulty. Given time, the ingredients that enter into the makeup of a habit or a prejudice become built into each other, so to speak. Psychiatrists know how difficult or impossible it is to break up such highly systematic affairs as neuroses and psychoses. A system of celestial bodies, held together by gravitational influences, may last for aeons. A social institution may last for centuries. What is involved in the case of the latter is this, that in every generation the behavior of almost every person born into and reared in a given community becomes organized in a certain way; it acquires a certain kind of pattern. The pattern generally becomes fixated.

Among the patterns acquired by a person born into and reared in or accepted into a group are stereotyped ideas. These ideas or idea-systems are either indoctrinated or unwittingly assimilated. They too tend to become fixated. They may and too often do dominate the mind to such an extent as to stand between it and reality. The fixation may be great enough to render the stereotyped idea or idea-system immune to logic or facts.

The cosmos itself appears to be a good example of a system composed of parts that fit into each other, sustain each other and perhaps the whole as well.

Change within a system is a response to disequilibrium. A system does not change for the sake of change, or in obedience to some principle of becoming. Change is therefore incidental. It is an aspect of the inner life of a system. When, because of inner or outer conditions, disequilibrium occurs, a reorientation of parts takes place. Or perhaps old parts are discarded and/or new elements added. The process continues until equilibrium is attained. Thus is becoming an aspect of being. There is becoming because being needs equilibrium.

It would seem from all this that the cosmos is fundamentally conservative. Being is conservative. But it is important to avoid one-sidedness. Being is also inventive and revolutionary. An entity may initiate change whenever change is necessary for survival or for the attainment of completeness of being.

❋ ❋ ❋ ❋

If now this is a universe in which entities enter into union, one must be prepared to discover that a number of factors will combine to produce a given result. Causation is multiple. An effect will be produced by the collaboration of two or more factors. People speak of this or that as being *the* cause, when they ought instead to speak of *a* cause. There probably is no such thing as *the* cause, unless it is the combination of all the factors productive of a given effect. Similarly, one hears of this or that as being *the* basic, fundamental, primary, central or most important aspect, *the* key, *the* crux, *the* heart of something or other. It may be proper to refer to an aspect as *a* basic, fundamental, primary, central or important fact. **The** basic fact about an entity is often its parts and the way they are organized into a whole.

The selection of some one factor as the cause, or of some aspect as basic, may be the result of ignorance or it may be prompted by bias. As a preceding chapter has pointed out, too close an attachment to a school of thought may involve such selectiveness. A school of thought is generally built around some selected aspect or portion of reality, the object of selection being dubbed basic, central, primary, fundamental. Too close an attachment to a school of thought thus makes it difficult to attain to a total view of things. The latter is equally difficult to attain for the group patriot—the person whose primary loyalty is to a group. This inability to attain to a total view is one of the causes of group conflict. As preceding chapters have shown, group conflict and the collective egotism of the group operate to hinder the group patriot from acquiring completeness of being. The group patriot and the person who is too closely attached to a school of thought are therefore likely to suffer from arrested growth.

*   *   *   *

If now entities enter into union, and if a number of factors merge to produce a given result, than an exceedingly important consequent follows. It is this, that it is possible to obtain a great many new things by putting entities together in novel and different ways. New combinations, new ways of union, of organization, novel patterns, may mean new effects, novel products, inventions. Artists, inventors, biologists, chemists and emergent evolutionists have known this for a long time. It is no mere theory. It has been proved by practice. This leads to the thought that, within limits, human beings can produce any kind of human being and human society they want. It may be possible, by appropriate combinations of biological, endocrinological, psychological and social factors to facilitate the emergence and growth of a more cooperative, democratic, sympathetic, rational, loving and magnanimous personality. It may thus be possible to increase the number and proportion of civilizers. It may thus be possible to augment and indefinitely sustain civilization.

This does not presuppose a rigid determinism. It is not being asserted that better human beings and a superior civilization can be produced with the same facility with which technologists produce a new machine or a new chemical. But every personality is, in part, a resultant of the union and operation of many factors, inner and outer. Any alteration and re-arrangement of these factors cannot fail to affect the result to some extent. Here indeed is a challenge to the men and women of today and tomorrow.

15

THE DIVINE POSSIBILITY

It was pointed out in the preceding chapter that one of the things that make for the persistence of an entity is the fact of organization. It was stated that when entities unite to form a larger and more inclusive entity, they may reenforce and strengthen each other; they then conserve each other's being, as well as that of the larger entity itself. Thus, by becoming organized, an entity becomes an institution, a fixation, so to speak.

The cosmos itself appears to be the expression of a passion for unity. Everything seems to be in search of other things to unite with. Nothing in the universe seems to prefer isolation. Gravitational influence may very well be the physical expression of a more fundamental urge. Everything seems to attract and be attracted to.

It is necessary to avoid one-sidedness. Attraction is not the whole story. There is also such a thing as repulsion. Things repel and are repelled. However, an entity does not repel out of a preference for isolation. It repels a given entity because of a preference for union with another entity. The urge is for unity, rather than isolation.

Again, while it is true that there are such things as organization and creation, it is equally true that there is such a thing as dissolution. At the same time that new entities are forming, other entities are breaking up. However, the elements that enter into the makeup of a dissolved entity do not as a rule remain in isolation. They seek out other elements and unite with them to form new wholes. Though dissolution may be as universal and as eternal a fact as unification, the two can hardly be said to exist on the same level. One may conceive the universe to exist in order that things might be created; one can hardly conceive the universe to exist in order that things might dissolve. One may envisage the cosmos as the expression of a unifying urge; one can hardly envisage the cosmos as the expression of an urge toward dissolution. Dissolution appears to be an incident in the history of unification.

Consider once more the apparent fact of reality subsisting on the following levels: inanimate matter, viruses, one-celled organisms, cell colonies, plants, conscious animals, human beings, civilizers. These eight levels or kinds of being are not compartmented off or insulated

against each other. They attract each other, enter into each other;
they work together. All these levels in their interaction make up the
cosmos.

When one considers the fact of this interaction and when one
bears in mind the presence in the cosmos of attraction, organization,
pattern, structure, unity and wholeness, one is led to ask whether
all this may not be the expression of an ultimate, universal and eternal
organizing factor. The existence of such a factor can be neither
proved nor disproved. Nevertheless, if the existence of this power
is assumed, the cosmos seems to become a somewhat more intelligible
affair. It ceases to be something that just is, and is for no reason
at all. It acquires flavor and spirit. It acquires some sort of significance and meaning, a significance and a meaning vaster and
deeper than the local and transient ones that are to be found in the
merely human. The latter itself, like everything else in the cosmos,
becomes an expression of this ultimate power. The highest level
of being known to humans, civilization, defined as the creation and
appreciation of ethical, aesthetic, intellectual and religious values,
becomes the highest empirically apprehensible expression of the
ultimate. Participation in such creation and appreciation becomes
the highest form of human activity. The creators of these values
become very important persons, perhaps the most important persons,
and their profession the most important of all.

This is, of course, all speculative. There may be such an ultimate
factor, and there may not be. If there is such a power, it may be
loving and intelligent, and it may not be.

The conception of an ultimate factor has occupied the minds of
men and women as far back as human memory can go. The thought
has been voiced by poets, prophets and philosophers, theologians and
teachers, metaphysicians and artists. They have sensed, or thought
they sensed, the presence of a power that makes for unity, integrity,
form, completeness, wholeness. They have called it by a variety of
names; among these have been creator, maker, idea, nisus toward
wholeness, law, love, God.

The problem lies beyond the capacity of the human mind to solve.
The human mind can go so far and no farther. Beyond that there
is nothing left but hope. The hope is something to cling to; one
should never let go of it. It may not be much, but there is nothing
better available. Hope should never be lost. One should make the
most of it. The organizing factor is, after all, a possibility, even a
probability; this power may well be an intelligent and loving power.